The Politics of Salvation:
THE HEGELIAN IDEA OF THE STATE

SUNY Series in Hegelian Studies
Quentin Lauer, Editor

The Politics of Salvation:
THE HEGELIAN IDEA OF THE STATE

Paul Lakeland

State University of New York Press
ALBANY

For T. F. L., M. M. L., and F. B. P.

Published by
State University of New York Press, Albany

© 1984 State University of New York

Printed in the United States of America

For information, address State University of New York
Press, State University Plaza, Albany, N.Y., 12246

Library of Congress Cataloging in Publications Data

Lakeland, Paul, 1946-
    The politics of salvation.

    (SUNY series in Hegelian studies)
    Bibliography: p.
    Includes index.
    1. Hegel, Georg Wilhelm Friedrich, 1770-1831—
Political science. 2. Hegel, Georg Wilhelm Friedrich,
1770-1831—Religion. 3. State, The. 4. Religion—
History—19th century. I. Title. II. Series.
JC233.H46L34 1984   310'.01'0924   83-17875
ISBN 0-87395-846-2
ISBN 0-87395-847-0 (pbk.)

10 9 8 7 6 5 4 3 2 1

Contents

Preface and Acknowledgments

The text of this book is already so long, and in places necessarily so closely argued, that I am loathe to ask my readers to wade through a lengthy preface too. This will be short and succint.

There are, of course, many people to thank for their assistance and advice on this project, although mentioning their names shall not imply that they agree with anything said here, or indeed that they necessarily think the project a good idea at all. In the first place, I must renew my thanks to Professors Peter C. Hodgson and Edward Farley of Vanderbilt University, where most of the research that went into the writing of this book was conducted. I want also to thank those of my peers at Vanderbilt between 1978 and 1980 who formed the *ad hoc* "Bible and Theology Discussion Group," and who suffered valiantly through some of the first formulations of opinions expressed here. Next on the list, a word of gratitude to my colleagues in the Religious Studies Department here at Fairfield University, in particular to Professors John E. Thiel and Alfred F. Benney, whose support and companionship help to create such a congenial working environment. My thanks go also to Professor Quentin Lauer, S.J., the editor of the series in which the book now appears, and finally to Beth Palmer, who uncomplainingly typed the final copy of the manuscript.

The second set of points I wish to make concerns the quotations from the writings of Hegel that occur frequently throughout the presentation. I have not sought to improve on the translations of either T. M. Knox or Peter C. Hodgson, but all other translations are my own work. Quotations from Knox's translation of the *Philosophy of Right* appear by kind permission of the Oxford University Press. The major variation in my translation from that of the principal translators of Hegel's works is that I have chosen to retain the German word *Geist*, rather than rendering it as either "mind" or "spirit." It is clear to me that neither of the two English words conveys the full richness of meaning of the German word, and it seems excusable in an academic context to employ a word which would be unacceptable in a more popular work. I have failed to be entirely consistent, however, as I have felt obliged to translate *geistlich* as "spiritual," and I have not been happy with "finite *Geists*," preferring "finite spirits." One can only forgive oneself so much maltreatment of the English language.

Finally, a point about language. I fully understand the position of those writers who feel that, regrettably, they cannot attempt the thoroughly non-sexist use of language. There are indeed some serious difficulties with the use of non-sexist language of God; should we say "God itself" or "Godself," for example? More generally, "his or her" and "he or she" can seem clumsy. Nevertheless, it seems to me that one can no longer simply relinquish the struggle for consistently non-sexist language. I have tried to be consistent without being clumsy, with what success it is for others to judge. Once again, it seems to me that a work which is in any case trying to break new *material* ground, is an appropriate medium for a little *formal* innovation. I have carried this principle as far as I thought possible; that is to say, in my own translations of Hegel, I have taken the liberty of letting Hegel too speak in non-sexist language, emboldened by the certainty that *Mensch* is most properly translated as "person" or "human being." I am confident that this nowhere entails an unsatisfactory representation of Hegel's thought.

P.F.L.

Fairfield University
Fairfield, Connecticut

List of Abbreviations

The abbreviations listed here are those which occur most often in the text. The practice adopted throughout is to give a reference to the work, quoting the paragraph number in the case of the Enc. and PR, and to follow that reference with a citation of the page number in the appropriate German and English texts, the latter even in those cases where the translation is my own.

Enc. *System der Philosophie* or "Encyclopaedia of the Philosophical Sciences." Vols. 8–10 in SW.

Hodgson *The Christian Religion*. Edited and translated by Peter C. Hodgson. AAR Texts and Translations Series, no. 2. Missoula, Montana: Scholars Press, 1979.

Hoff. *Grundlinien der Philosophie des Rechts*. Edited by Johannes Hoffmeister. Hamburg: Felix Meiner Verlag, 1969.

Knox *Hegel's Philosophy of Right*. Translated with notes by T. M. Knox. London: Oxford University Press, 1967.

Lasson *Vorlesungen über die Philosophie der Religion*. Edited by Georg Lasson. 4 vols. in two. Hamburg: Felix Meiner Verlag, 1925–30.

LPH *The Philosophy of History*. Translated by J. Sibree, with a preface by Charles Hegel, and a new introduction by C. J. Friedrich. New York: Dover, 1956.

LPR *Lectures on the Philosophy of Religion*. 3 vols. Translated by E. B. Speirs and J. B. Sanderson. New York: Humanities Press, 1962.

PM *Hegel's Philosophy of Mind, Being Part Three of the Encyclopaedia of the Philosophical Sciences* (1830). Translated by William Wallace, together with the *Zusätze* in Boumann's text (1845), translated by A. V. Miller, with a foreword by J. N. Findlay. Oxford: Clarendon Press, 1971.

PR *Grundlinien der Philosophie des Rechts*. SW vol. 7.

SW *Sämtliche Werke: Jubiläumsausgabe in zwanzig Bänder*. Edited by Hermann Glockner. Stuttgart, Fr. Frommanns Verlag, 1958.

VPG *Vorlesungen über die Philosophie der Weltgeschichte*. SW, vol. 11.

VPR *Vorlesungen über die Philosophie der Religion*. SW, vols. 15–16.

HEGEL
AND LIBERATIVE PRAXIS

I f this introduction had been entitled "Kant and Jogging" or "Spinoza and the Low-Fat Diet," it might have raised no more eyebrows than the association of radically post-Marxist Christian thought with one of Karl Popper's leading enemies of the "open society." In the English-speaking world, and especially outside the ranks of genuine Hegel scholars, the great idealist philosopher is thought of, if at all, as the philosopher of Prussianism and of abstraction; he is suspect of encouraging totalitarianism, he is seen as an advocate of war as a supreme national activity, he may even be thought of as anti-semitic, and he is certainly abstruse.

The particular focus of this book on Hegel's concept of the state may seem to be asking for even more trouble. After all, wasn't Hegel the man who sought to subordinate the will of the individual to the almighty state—thus making him the forerunner of national socialism at least, if not of Soviet-style communism? How is it possible to take this particular philosopher and his state, and to make a case for that idea of the state as a key factor in a political theology proclaiming human liberation? Evidently, the picture of Hegel presented is going to be different from the caricature above.

The Hegel found in these pages is not a totalitarian thinker. Instead, we shall see Hegel in a far more defensible fashion, as the last metaphysician, perhaps the last great Christian philosopher. Feuerbach and Marx both knew this to be the correct interpretation of the master, and, from their own perspectives, rightly reacted against it.

But just because he is a genuinely Christian thinker, it is really otiose to seek to label him as conservative or liberal or reactionary. At times in details he is all of these things: in other details, he is distinctly progressive. But such labels only belong to political ideologues, where Hegel is in the true sense of the word a radical thinker. He can express views at both ends of the political spectrum simply because the political and social opinions are merely applications of a view of the world which goes far deeper. This fundamental and thoroughgoing metaphysic is also one which, frankly, is not really comprehensible without some appreciation of Christian theology. The symbolism of Christian trinitarian and incarnational theology, and the logic of the Hegelian dialectic, mutually interpenetrate and strengthen one another.

This, then, is the justification for the ensuing investigation. If Hegel can be understood (as he frequently expressed himself) as expressing conceptually in speculative philosophy what religion expresses in the form of image and representation, then it would seem that the covenantal demands of justice and freedom from oppression, the Christian struggle for a free and authentic humanity, and Christian hope in the kingdom of God, will all find their counterpart in the Hegelian system. If this is so, and I believe it is, then a Hegelian political theology should be able to illuminate the connections between the expectation of salvation and the struggle for liberation. By so doing, it ought in passing to draw classical theological thinking (which Hegel utilized) and contemporary religious thought a little closer together.

At the same time it has to be said that many of those whose works have inspired this one would be impatient of its purpose. Latin American liberation theologians do not, as a breed, look kindly on theorisers, especially on those who write from the comfort of (relatively) affluent ivory towers. On the contrary, they insist that liberative praxis in solidarity with the oppressed is the indispensable condition for authentic religion and responsible theology, since it is the only way to avoid the subtle distortions of ideological presuppositions.[1] The Christian in the liberationist perspective is enjoined to faith as a prereflective commitment to God's poor, out of which will grow a Christ-like identification with those whom the world has marginalized and a living appreciation of what it means to cooperate in building the kingdom. The religion of the "developed" world, and especially its traditional theology, is relegated to the ranks of the purely theoretical.

Because the criticism of Western theology is based on its lack of liberative praxis, the same critique extends even to the European and North American variant on liberation theology that goes by the name of "political theology" pure and simple. It is attacked by liberation theologians not so much for what it says as for its lack of a practical basis on which to say it. To the liberation theologian, theory is not wrong in itself; but if it is not the construction of a theology as a reflection on personal liberative praxis, it is empty abstraction. However, the complexity of the issue consists precisely in the fact that in societies where marginalization is more subtle and where the object of a prereflective commitment is more difficult to identify, authentic liberative praxis may look a little different from that in Latin America. It is even possible that political theology itself could be one form of liberative praxis, under certain conditions.[2]

The work of a European theologian upon the discipline of political theology may be liberative if it unshackles the mind from presuppositions and hidden ideological biases and in fact frees the individual to make the leap of commitment. Dorothee Soelle's act of defining political theology can be a step in the achievement of a revolutionary consciousness on the part of her readers:

> Political theology is . . . a theological hermeneutic which, in distinction from a theology that interprets reality from an ontological or existentialist point of view, holds open an horizon of interpretation in which politics is understood as the comprehensive and decisive sphere in which Christian truth should become praxis.[3]

In itself, the intellectual conversion liberates nothing more than the mind. But the point about political theology itself is that it leads inexorably back to action (praxis) in the human world (the *polis*). The further question, and one of the root questions of this present work, is whether the "political praxis" that stands in some as yet undefined dialectical relationship to theological reflection, can be equated with or related to what is traditionally referred to as salvation.

Political theology, aside from the predominantly German school which happens to bear this name, I take to be a generic term, of which theology of liberation is the best-known species. All political theologians, then, subscribe to the axiom that "praxis is the realm of salvation." For Segundo or Gutierrez, this means that the kingdom is built up in solidarity with the marginalized and oppressed.[4] For Soelle or Metz, it means that it is in the political sphere broadly understood that the gospel message must convince.[5] The phrase, "praxis is the realm of salvation," implies in itself no commitment to a particular interpretation of the term praxis, although it obviously involves doing rather than merely being, and it says only that through this praxis the Christian is brought into touch with that which is important for salvation. It leaves open the option of interpreting it to mean that liberative praxis is salvation, or that liberative praxis merits salvation, or that through identification with the marginalized we come to be sensitive to the call of God to repentance, and so on. All these possibilities make the link between doing—in some way cooperating in "building the kingdom"—and the concept of salvation. Salvation is itself, of course, something of an umbrella term—conviction of justification, membership in God's grace-filled community, achieving full humanity, becoming more fully the person I am, and so on. They all nevertheless draw "liberation" and "salvation" into close relationship, if not identity.

Fully human behaviour is the instinctive response to a situation which response, on reflection, is susceptible of rational defence. We act out of our full humanity, and can later recognize that our action was fully human. Had we stopped first to analyze which action would be fully human, the moment would have slipped by and we should in any case have acted out of a one-sided intellectual conviction. This is why the liberation theologians' definition of faith as a prereflective commitment to the oppressed is fundamentally accurate. Faith is an attitude in which believers find themselves when they reflect upon what they take to be of absolute importance in their lives, not a code they establish *a priori*, and out of which they then measure their permissible passions. Even to say this is of course already the beginnings of an intellectualization of the faith-impulse, but so long as the intellectualization is descriptive rather than prescriptive, its necessity and inevitability is a function of human reason.

Can we be similarly rational and descriptive about the claim that "praxis is the realm of salvation?" In itself, it is a totally unexceptional axiom, if it is taken to mean that what we do is the true test of what we are. Moreover, particularly clearly in poorer countries, although perhaps no less true in countries like our own, instinctive association with the less fortunate is more truly Christ-like than playing the political system or living a quiet life in the lee of the parish church. The claim that "praxis is the realm of salvation" *feels* right, and that is not a negligible factor in stating the case for its *being* right. But it is not the whole case. In this work, then, I set out to provide a coherent theological and intellectual justification, in classical theological and philosophical categories, for the clarion call of political theology: praxis is the realm of salvation.

The trail along which I have chosen to seek this "theology of praxis" leads through the often tangled jungle of the mature Hegel's thought to a philosophical theology heavily dependent on his theory of the state. This may be a surprising choice of direction to some, and although a full defence of it must be sought in the argument of the book as a whole, a few preliminary remarks may coax the sceptic at least a little way along my path.

The key to the association of Hegelian thought with the search for an intellectual justification for praxis as the realm of salvation, lies in the notion of incarnation. This we have already briefly noted above. I shall argue, on the one hand, that incarnation is *the* motif of Hegelian *Religions-philosophie*. Many greater thinkers have preceded me in this. But I shall seek to show further that this motif extends to the notion of the state. The role of the community of finite spirits in seeking to realize the idea of the state in given historical epochs is the "horizontal" counterpart of the worshipping community of the Church. Both together constitute religion, not merely the latter. More importantly, the possibility of recognizing this lies in the notion of incarnation, that seed planted in Christendom which for Hegel finally bears fruit in the activity of speculative philosophy. Only in the light of a theology of the incarnation can we construct an anthropology of sufficient sublimity that a "secular" activity like the realization of the state can truly be a sacred thing.

It will be argued, on the one hand, that political theology broadly conceived only makes sense from an incarnational perspective. Political action can only be "building the kingdom" when there is some reason to consider human beings as divine agents, and, saving an anthropomorphic or magical idea of religion, this is only possible given some ontological conceptualization of salvation. In other words, if incarnational theology makes it possible to view authentic human action as, so to speak, God's work in the world, then that which builds a more fully human world brings the world closer to God. Hegel's idea of the state is instantiated or actualized only in a circular process, in which the human activity to realize the corporate ideal is in fact strengthened and even made possible by the corporate ideal itself. The idea of the state fuels the human agents in whom and only in whom it has any actuality. The principle of the incarnation, we might say, is the spark which ignites the combustion of God's work in the world. Thus, if liberative praxis can be identified with the actualization of the idea of the state, and it seems that it can, then the sociopolitical growth that occurs through it is at one and the same time a growth in individual and corporate humanity towards an ontology of human nature which only makes sense in the light of the Incarnation.

This work might be considered a "reconstruction" of Hegel's idea of the state, in the sense of the word intended by Jürgen Habermas:

> . . . *Reconstruction* signifies taking a theory apart and putting it back together again in a new form in order to attain more fully the goal it has set for itself. This is the normal way . . . of dealing with a theory that needs revision in many respects but whose potential for stimulation has still not been exhausted.[6]

Hegel's goal was the assertion of the fulfillment of the speculative appropriation of truth. In my opinion he did not make it sufficiently clear that it was the *speculative* appropriation with which he was concerned. Hence, the number of misreadings of Hegel as an absolutist, or as a proponent of the Prussian state as the arrival of heaven on earth. In actual fact, he really claimed only that the intellectual tools for the perfection of society were now available. Thus he might even be able to sidestep a hermeneutic of suspicion, since the problem of a false consciousness, although it might well warp judgment, could not in the end triumph over the all-pervasive human reference to reason, without which nothing at all could be said. This is not the least of the ways in which Hegel has connections with transcendental thinkers.

The reconstruction attempted here is simply that involved in reading an early nineteenth century thinker with a late twentieth century mind. The probblem of history and the hermeneutical role of the interpreter and his or her prejudices cannot simply be ignored. Nor can the elements of degeneration in society and civilization, upon which Hegel did not dwell, be swept under the carpet in the name of a tidy theory. But that this book is a reconstruction rather than a post-Hegelian fairy tale, will be demonstrated if the truth of my conviction is born out, namely, that there is nothing here false to Hegel, and nothing which is not stimulated by reflection on his words.

Turning to a few points of detail, it is necessary first to stress that various layers must be identified in reading Hegel's works—above all, we might say, the roles of the characters in the drama and that of the narrator, as well as the point of view of the audience. Human history, for example, is at one level simply what it appears to be, an enormously complex interweaving of human actions and emotions, with seemingly chance happenings. That this is seen by Hegel as the material upon which reason works to produce the true social process that we might call essential history,[7] does not mean that all or even some of the participants in everyday events are aware of any more than their own immediate concerns. The characters in the drama do not know that they are in a play, still less which act is in progress, or which of them has the "lead" and which are bit-parts. Such distinctions are available only to the onlookers. The Hegelian spectator stands at the end of history (in the sense of culmination if not of final moment), and simply by virtue of being at that point has the chance to recapitulate, to synthesize, to appropriate and to understand. Speculative philosophy, the Hegelian point of view, is no more than the adequate description of the truly actual in history, the delineation of necessity at work in contingency.

To give a practical illustration of how inadvertence to this distinction can be confusing, we need only look in a preliminary fashion at the role of religion in human society. When the speculative philosopher interprets religion as knowing the truth, but not knowing that the truth is the truth (which is reserved to the speculative viewpoint), the claim is simply that the characters in the drama do not understand the dynamic of the plot. It would be a misunderstanding to imagine that Hegel was saying, for example, that there was somehow imperfection in the acceptance of religion as religion in human history, or that religion would die out now that the high point of its speculative transformation had been reached. On the other hand, the interpreter of the truth of things could not settle for the representative level of religion, but must press on to uncover the truth of that representation.

A further complexity must be noted. A study of Hegel's view of the state not only involves us in examining how he describes the truth of something which, if it exists at all, exists in history, but also in distancing ourselves from that description. If speculative philosophy interprets history, what interprets speculative philosophy? Since that speculative philosophy has now become history, perhaps our metadiscipline might be philosophy of history. But that speculative philosophy is or was a philosophy, and so perhaps it would be truer to describe what we are doing as history of philosophy. If we were to stop at description, we might be happier to consider our research under the heading of "history of ideas." Whichever we choose, what matters is to recognize that it constitutes a third literary or narrative level of the process. In the ensuing pages it will be important always to distinguish if we are walking into battle with Napoleon, immortalizing him as a world-historical individual with Hegel, or comparing such an interpretation with a Tolstoyian promotion of chance.

It is also important to note that the word "state" (*Staat*) can itself be misleading. We shall have to recall more than once that Hegel was not anxious to identify his notion of the state with that of any existent state, still less with the political structure of his own Prussia. The state for Hegel is an ideal which each successvie age brings about insofar as it goes beyond mere socioeconomic interdependence to a conception of an organic, rationally ordered community, an ethical whole governed by reason. In this community, the good of the whole is by definition the good of the individual. This is not and perhaps never can be fully actual in history. The perfection of the ideal is reserved for the realm of speculative philosophy; there it is perfect, because it is perfectly conceived. But the truth, though not intellectually grasped, perhaps, is instantiated in every social organism to a greater or lesser extent.

There are good reasons, then, why we perhaps ought to avoid using the word "state" to translate Hegel's *Staat*. Without the qualification introduced in the preceding paragraph, its use will certainly mislead the reader. What Hegel means by "civil society" is what most moderns understand by "state." Nevertheless, I have chosen to retain the word "state." If we were to replace it by some other, then the critical function of state over against civil society (the socioeconomic convenience) would be lost. Indeed, civil society would pass for "the state" and Hegel's point is that it is no such thing. Hegel wishes to reserve (and so preserve) the word "state" for the true community which will re-present with modern complexity the naive unity of the Athenian model. The state is the ethical whole which exists wherever rights and duties are perfectly balanced.

The fact that this book has a foot in two quite distinct camps, finally, entails a certain complexity to its structure. It is at one and the same time a study of Hegel and a contribution to the intellectual stiffening of political theology. It is to be hoped, therefore, that it has something to say to the Hegelian, perhaps contributing to his or her understanding of the Christian presuppositions and character of Hegel's thought. It is equally to be wished that the political theologians will find it stimulating in their search for a framework for an often haphazard discipline. And it would not be the least value of this work if the two groups were able to learn a little about one another. There are structural tensions in such an enterprise, but there are benefits to its successful conclusion.

Chapter I

THE STATE IN THE SYSTEM

H egel's conception of the state is treated in a large number of studies.[1] The majority of these works give some attention to the origins of Hegel's state,[2] its early and uncertain appearance in the *älteste Systementwurf*,[3] and its more confident showings in the writings of the so-called "Jena period."[4] As readers of the introduction will realize, such a step-by-step procedure is neither necessary nor appropriate here. Our concern is not so much with whence Hegel derived his idea of the state, nor with the stages towards its more perfect expression, but with its pivotal place in the system as a whole. In Hegel's state, the institution and the human being are most closely allied; politics is given a human face, and the human is rendered inescapably political by the close association of finite Geist and objective Geist. But this is to anticipate too much.

It is because we are principally concerned with the place of the state in the system that in this study we will turn immediately to the mature treatment of the state found in two places, namely, the *Encyclopaedia of the Philosophical Sciences*[5] and the *Philosophy of Right*.[6] We cannot, of course, ignore the earlier writings, and from time to time we shall have to refer back to the younger Hegel for clarification. Nevertheless, our main concern is not with this development, nor with one or more of the various accusations made against Hegel's state — of "Prussianism," conservatism, totalitarianism, among others — but rather with an understanding of what idea is at the heart of the state, beneath the historically conditioned details in which he expresses it. Hegel's idea can of course only be actualized in history, but that is not to say that every detail constitutes the actualization of the idea. To use terms unfamiliar in the Hegelian lexicon, the essence may need to be informed, but the form is never adequate to the essence.[7]

As human beings, our investigation clearly takes place within the limitations of human history. Human history can be described, I take it, as the actions and reactions of human subjects as they construct and maintain a human world within the framework of the natural world. The concrete structures of human existence are what Hegel refers to as "objective Geist," while the human subjects are finite Geist or finite spirits.[8] Clearly, any philosophical system works through the limitations of the human mind, and thankfully Hegel's is no excepetion. It belongs, however, to that group of philosophies which from the inevitably limited perspective of human history struggle to comprehend the place of human history within a framework of meaning which goes beyond it, and the place of human nature in a conception of reality which overreaches it. The meaning of history and the meaning of human beings lie beyond them, in some sense. The Hegelian system is in other words truly metahistorical, metaphysical and, in the deepest meaning of the word, religious. The viability of this perspective is dependent on the assumption (which we shall discuss shortly) that the whole is somehow present in the realm of human history. Otherwise we should be trapped in the Kantian dichotomy between appearance and reality. If Geist is taken to be reality itself, then both objective Geist and finite spirits must both be and not be identical to it. Identity without difference would involve the reduction of Hegel's vision either to materialism or pantheism: difference without identity implies philosophical (or at lease metaphysical) agnosticism.

This general problematic is particularly relevant to the place of the state, which in Hegelian parlance can be described as the highest actualization of Geist in human history. Above all other institutions, the state is in principle the most fully rational. It is the pinnacle of objective Geist. It is also the culmination of the truly ethical activity of human beings. But for all this to be enlightening we need to delve more fully into the general framework of Hegel's thinking. We will approach the state indirectly, tracing Hegel's reasoning through his discussion of objective Geist. Before we do that, however, we need to say a little more about the notion of Geist in general.

Hegel's *Encyclopaedia* is really the only completed systematic enterprise of his entire career, and it was intended to be introductory. It is best read, therefore, alongside those fuller treatments of the same or similar material. Part one of the *Encyclopaedia*, the so-called "lesser" logic, is illumined by a parallel study of the *Wissenschaft der Logik*,[9] and the treatment of objective Geist in Part Three is amplified by the *Philosophy of Right*, if not also by the lecture series on the philosophy of history[10] and the philosophy of religion.[11] In the following discussion, therefore, our focus will be on the second principle section of the third part of the *Encyclopaedia*,[12] which treats of objective Geist, and on the considerable expansion of the same material throughout the *Philosophy of Right*.

If objective Geist is our concern, it behooves us to say something about the nature of Geist in general. We ought not, however, to phrase the issue quite so casually, since Hegel warns us that "knowledge of Geist is the most concrete, and therefore the most exalted and most difficult of knowledge."[13] In fact, knowledge of Geist is neither empty theorizing nor description of appearance, but knowledge of what is as such, in-and-for-itself. Within the development of thought in the *Encyclopaedia*, Geist only makes its appearance with self-consciousness. The first part (the Logic) has dealt with the logical Idea, with, we might say, the internal necessity of the dialectical process, or the structure of the concept. The work as a whole delineates the way in which that internal necessity comes to know itself as the structure of reality. Geist is knowledge (the concept) which knows itself to be knowledge. The second part of the *Encyclopaedia* follows the progress of the Idea through nature, in a painfully precise demonstration that the internal rational necessity of the logical Idea is the underlying structure of nature.[14] Now nature conforms to a rational order, at least if Hegel's depiction is accepted, but it is not rational itself, since it lacks self-consciousness. Self-consciousness makes its appearance in the system with the appearance of Geist, but in finite Geist, or finite human beings who demonstrate the actualization of Geist in their capacity for reflection and self-consciousness.

In the cognitional order, Geist is then first encountered in finite human individuals who know themselves. But such self-knowledge must not stop at "a self-knowledge through the particular talents, character, inclinations and foibles of individuals."[15] In reflection upon self, finite Geist comes to see itself as an actualization of the logical Idea—indeed, as the self-actualization of the Idea. The concept, the structure of rationality itself, is perceived in its logical completeness by the finite human being, who also sees that same logic expressed in the order of nature, operative in the very process of coming to know, and actual in the act of knowing. Thus, the logical Idea is revealed to be, when actualized, Geist. Geist is the self-comprehending Idea:

> Every act of Geist is thus only a comprehending of itself, and so the aim of all true science is simply this: that Geist knows itself in everything in heaven and on earth.[16]

The point of realization that Geist is itself the truth of what is is reserved, however for the final section of the *Philosophy of Geist* (part three of the *Encyclopaedia*). This section discusses "absolute" Geist, although, of course, the realization that Geist is the truth of what is, is a realization of finite concrete individuals, of finite Geist within the realm of objective Geist. Here, as elsewhere in Hegel's philosophy, the procedure is circular:

> Actual Geist, which is the entire subject-matter of the science of Geist, has external nature for its proximate, and the logical Idea for its first, presupposition. The philosophy of nature must have as its result (and so Logic by mediation) the proof of the necessity of the concept of Geist. The science of Geist for its part must authenticate this concept through its development and actualization. So what we say here in the form of an assertion at the beginning of our treatment of it, can only be proved scientifically through the whole of philosophy. All we can do here is elucidate the concept of Geist for the imagination.[17]

For the modern mind, the problem of conceptualizing Geist is that the clearest images for what Hegel had in mind come out of the symbol-system of the Christian tradition. Unfortunately, those images are increasingly unfamiliar to philosophers, as they are to littérateurs, scientists, and the public at large. In consequence, it is a not unusual phenomenon that studies of Hegel will treat him with the greatest respect, quarrying the corpus for insights on this or that, while dismissing his central notion of Geist.[18] However, if we have recourse to the theological symbols of trinity or incarnation, notions which Hegel himself uses frequently, this ought not to be taken as evidence of an unreconstructed "right-wing" Hegelianism which would see him simply as an apologist for a variant of Christianity. As the later chapter on the relation of religion and philosophy will show, although the truth is materially present in both disciplines, it is philosophy which is formally appropriate to the knowledge of truth as truth.[19]

In spite of the above warnings, a moment's attention to classical trinitarian theology does shed light on Hegel's conception of Geist. In the order of human cognition, awareness of God as Trinity comes to the orthodox Christian through revelation. God is revealed as Father, Son and Spirit in human history, as creator, as redeemer, and as the ongoing presence of the divine in history. If trinitarian theology comes to know the three "subsistences" of God by their activity or presence in human history, the human mind can then go on to infer that, if revelation does not play us false (and how could it), this trio of subsistences perceived at work in history must correspond to something in the nature of God. In other words, the "economy of salvation" follows the pattern of the self-expression of God. God's internal completeness is already trinitarian from all eternity; if God chooses to create and ultimately to redeem, this will occur as the self-expression of the triune God.

Hegel persistently claimed that his philosophy was based on experience. Thus, we need to attend to objective Geist as the starting point in the cognitional order. The dialectic of Geist is only evident in human history, though it is affirmed as the structure of reality as a whole. Cognitionally, then, we can say that the dialectic of Geist evident in history (the chronological dialectic) is to the structure of the concept (the logical dialectic) as the economic is to the immanent trinity. They are identical, although they subsist differently; the one occupies the field of logic and expresses the universal structure of human knowing, the other demonstrates this structure at work in history.

The ins-and-outs of this particular parallelism will be discussed in more detail in the chapter on religion (Chap. III). However, it seems appropriate at this point to consider briefly what understanding of necessity might be active in the relation of the moments of the dialectic. The first is non-controversial; just as it is clearly necessary that if God shall act, it shall be according to the divine nature, so the concept as the structure of knowing shall be that according to which all individual acts of knowing are ordered. But the question arises: although the structure of knowing provides the pattern for acts of knowing, through which self-knowledge or self-consciousness is reached, does this not mean in its turn that the achievement of self-consciousness is dependent upon individual acts of knowing? It is hard to avoid answering this in the affirmative, but then we are forced to the further question, whether this does not make Absolute Geist dependent on finite Geist and, on the trinitarian parallel, whether this does not represent God as dependent on that which God has created? Quentin Lauer, in dialogue with Michael Theunissen, makes the following suggestion:

> The point is one that Hegel had made much earlier in the *Encyclopaedia*: that it is only *in* thought and *as* thought, that spiritual being, including that of God, can make sense. God, then, can be object of thought and thought alone, which does not mean that there must be finite thought, if God is to *be*; rather it means that if God is to be *for* finite spirit, He must be for finite spirit as *thinking*.[20]

Expressed in the terminology of Christian theology, this would mean accepting that God in self does *not* need creation, but that having created, the perfection of God in and for creation depends upon God's free self-subjection to creation. Given Trinity and Creation, can Incarnation be far behind?

We are, of course, more concerned with Hegel's Geist than we are with the Christian God, at least at this point. In fact, it seems to me that in the God-concepts of some contemporary theologies of hope and process there may be more chance of a place for Hegel's Geist than in classical trinitarian theology. But be that as it may, the point to emphasize here is that from the perspective of human beings in history, Geist comes to be absolute Geist, comes to know itself as Geist, in and through the knowing of finite Geist in the realm of objective Geist. Human history is the process of Geist's coming to self-consciousness. It is then a *necessary* moment in the dialectic of Geist, viewed from the human world.

Geist can also be clarified by attention to Hegel's epistemology. Hegel considers that conscious self-knowledge, or self-consciousness, is achieved through recognition of the object of knowledge as something other, and thus of self as something other than that which is known. The subject moves always from inchoate or unconscious, unmediated self-possession, to its negation in the knowledge of the other, to the negation of the other in the subject's idealization, and so to mediated and conscious knowledge of self. *The Philosophy of Nature*, the second part of the *Encyclopaedia*, deals with pure externality; external, that is, to "that actual self-existent inwardness which constitutes the essential nature of mind."[21] In other words, there is no consciousness in the realm of nature, no relationality and no freedom. The distinctiveness of Geist stems from its place at the point at which the otherness of the Idea is seen to be a moment only, and the process of return into itself of the Idea from the other is begun and accomplished. The essence of Geist, then, is *ideality*:

> This transformation of externality, which belongs to the concept of Geist, is that which we have called ideality. All the activities of Geist are nothing other than various forms of the return of externality to internality, which Geist itself is, and only through this return, through this idealization or assimilation of externality, does it become and is it Geist.[22]

Geist, then, which is variously described as self-consciousness, truth, freedom, and reason, has ideality for its concept or essence, in the sense that its goal is to reduce the logical idea to externality, or to comprehend what is. Geist is the principle of rationality, and the exercise of rationality must of its nature seek the reason of things: "To him who looks upon the world rationally, the world in its turn presents a rational aspect."[23]

Geist itself exhibits the same formal structure as the logical Idea, and as the structure of the Hegelian vision as a whole. At this point, we might recall the distinction referred to in the introduction, between the actor and the audience. Geist develops through three stages: ideality, objectivity, and the union of both, which is absolute truth. But in the first stage, this is not clear:

> Geist is certainly Geist from the beginning, but it does not know that it is Geist. Geist itself does not grasp its concept from the outset; it is only we who are watching who know its concept.[24]

To illustrate this, we can adopt the image of the growth of the child, an example Hegel himself uses here. A baby is only potentially or conceptually a rational being, but the entire reality is there *in nuce*. Subjective and objective Geist are both finite, but this finitude is only a moment in the true essence of Geist as "the Idea in the form of ideality." If Geist is this essentially, then it is essentially the negatedness of the finite:

> So in Geist the finite signifies only something transformed, not something essentially. Thence the true quality of Geist is much more to be the true infinite; that is, the infinite which does not simply stand opposed to the finite, but includes the finite in itself as a moment. So it is an empty phrase to say, "There are finite spirits." Geist as Geist is not finite, but contains the finite as something which is to be transformed, and which is transformed.[25]

The finitude of subjective and objective Geist has to do with their being determined, as, for example, in receiving another into consciousness. Yet this determination, this limitedness, involves knowing a limit, and knowing a limit as limit necessarily implies transcending the limit:

> Finitude, perceived truly, is, as we said, included in infinite, the limited included in the unlimited. Geist then is both infinite and finite, not only one or merely the other; in its perishing it remains infinite, because it surpasses the finite within it. Nothing in it is fixed, essential being, but rather everything is ideal, mere appearance. So, because God is Geist, God must determine self, posit finitude in self (otherwise God would be simply a dead, empty abstraction); but since the reality God gives to self in God's self-determination is fully conformable to God, God does not become finite. So the limitation is not in God and in Geist, but it is only posited by Geist in order to be surpassed.[26]

Throughout this work our concern is above all with objective Geist, the moment of human history. The institutions of our rational world are rational institutions, proceeding according to reason, but they possess their rationality in the mode of externality; that is, they do not know *that* they are moments in the absolute as it dwells in the territory of finitude. Only the philosophers, the speculative transformers of reality, are aware that objective Geist is what it is. But the fact that objective Geist is itself not aware of what it is, does not alter the reality, that it is what it is. There is a sense, for example, in which Hegel considers the state to be divine, to be the fullest actualization of Geist in the institutions of human history. This means not so much that any particular state is beyond criticism, but that any particular state is *the* state insofar as it is, through the subjective wills which comprise it, the concrete actualization of freedom in human history. There may be a sense in which history is itself divine, but the knowledge that it is so is the preserve of the philosophy of history. Religion is the most direct human approach to the divine reality, but that and how it is so is not revealed to religion, but to philosophy. Only in the concept is the truth of things known, and only absolute Geist grasps the concept as the concept, although all that "precedes" it counts as a series of moments in the development of the concept.

Objective Geist, the second section of the *Philosophy of Geist*, itself the third part of the *Encyclopaedia*, is also tripartite in structure. It moves from a consideration of abstract right, through subjective will or morality, to the union of abstract right and subjectivity, the ethical life. The treatment of the ethical life, in its turn, begins with the family, in which Geist "appears as feeling Geist"[27] and moves through the developed totality of the relation of individuals in a system of needs (civil society), to their harmonization in the state as the self-conscious ethical substance. The higher synthesis is achieved in bringing together the natural ethical sentiment of the family and its internal relationships (feeling) with the strictly structural conveniences of sociality. As a whole, then, this section deals with the sociopolitical dimensions of human history as the transition to absolute Geist.

The *Philosophy of Right* is nothing more than an expansion of the treatment of sociopolitical issues in the *Encyclopaedia*. Published in 1821, between the first and second editions of the *Encyclopaedia*

(1817, 1827), the *Philosophy of Right* is considerably longer than even the expanded treatment in the third edition of the *Encyclopaedia* (1830). Hegel himself described the *Philosophy of Right* as a textbook, "an enlarged and especially a more systematic exposition of the same fundamental concepts" contained in the *Encyclopaedia*.[28] The treatment of the subject-matter is not significantly altered in the PR, although expanded; so, for example, the extended treatment of the relation between state and individual in the *Zusatz* to §258 has no parallel in the *Encyclopaedia*, although it contradicts nothing there. In proceeding now to a brief outline of the path to the concept of the state, and the major features of the state, I shall follow the order of the *Encyclopaedia*, amplifying it by reference to the PR.

Objective Geist, since it is Geist, is a moment of the absolute Idea, that is, of the Idea having come to know itself as the truth of the logical Idea and externality (nature). But since it is *objective* Geist, it is this true self-knowledge only externally, i.e., expressed in institutions and human sociality in a form which is not itself conscious of itself.[29] Its most primitive or abstract form is as the actualization of the concept of right (*Recht*). Actualized in an individual, right is based in the purposive action of will, as it seeks to embody its freedom.[30] In this process, a human world is created:

> The basis of right is, in general, Geist; its precise place and point of origin is the will. The will is free, so that freedom is both the substance of right and its goal, while the system of right is the realm of freedom made actual, the world of Geist brought forth out of itself like a second nature.[31]

The English-speaking reader may have problems understanding Hegel's use of the term 'right'. Knox points out that Hegel meant the term to do for civil law, but also for morality, ethical life and world history.[32] In our discussions here, it is important to note that it will only mean "civil law" when that civil law truly conforms to the overriding ethical prescriptions. If it did not have unfortuante connotations too, the term 'natural law' might be a better translation of *Recht*, since it is undoubtedly the case for Hegel that the truth of civil law, morality, the ethical life and world history conforms to the rationality of the nature of Geist.[33]

Formally, freedom is actualized in the unity of the rational will with the individual will; this unity "is the immediate and unique element in which the former is actualized."[34] In other words, rationality and freedom are only actual in individual human wills in human history. This point will be worth recalling when Hegel's state is accused of being totalitarian or monolithic. In the dialectic of part and whole, although the individual is only truly free (i.e., acting according to his or her nature) when in conformity with the rational will (the abstract truth of freedom), the rational will has no actuality (i.e., existence in the world) above and apart from human action. The abstract truth is brought to be in and through human activity, and in the human action to actualize the rational will, bringing forth the world of Geist like a second nature, the rational will is shown to be not only the truth of the world, but the truth of the individual wills which bring it to be.

The first stage of the exercise of the freedom of the individual will is in the arbitrary appropriation of some external thing as "mine."[35] Property (*Eigenthum*) is understandably a word which calls to mind Marx's debt to Hegel, although it might be a mistake to exaggerate that debt in this precise respect, since Hegel's chief concern with property is his belief that it stands at the origin of personality. Geist in the finite individual is experienced as freedom and individuality in possession (*Besitz*). In making some external thing mine, I place my will within it (*meiner personlichen Willen in sie hineinlegen*), and thus is born the notion of property. Property as possession is a means, says Hegel, but as the existence of personality, it is an end in itself.[36] Yet the existence of my personality actually occurs in other persons, because for them my will is evident not as it is in me, as abstract, but as it is in my act of taking possession of what is mine, or even by designating it mine. Thus I am a person in virtue of saying "mine" (*die Repulsion meiner von mir selbst*), and concretely a person when heard to say "mine."[37]

The notion of the other becomes concrete in the step from property to contract. I choose something as mine arbitrarily, but once mine, it can only become not mine when I give it up or alienate it. In relinquishing something to another who takes it as his or hers, there is a relation established between wills. The rights of individuals over external things, and the right established in the notion of contract between individuals, creates the possibility of criminality, or the negation of right. Right or law is only real in the world, made actual through the instrumentality of the subjective will. It is possible for the subjective will to choose not to actualize the right, but this gives subjectivity no power over right as such. By being the individual's abdication of the role of instrumentality in actualizing the reasonable will. It has truth and reality only in actualizing right, which is its concept. Insofar as the will in itself realizes the reasonable will, it is *morality* proper.[38]

In the consideration of morality, turning now away from the notion of abstract right, we are concerned with the subjectivity of freedom:

> To have that right, the human being must possess a knowledge of the difference between good and evil; both ethical and religious principles shall not make a demand on someone simply as external laws and the prescriptions of authority, as something to be obeyed by someone, but have their assent, recognition and even foundation in the heart, feeling, conscience, intelligence, etc.[39]

But "the moral" does not simply mean "the good." "Moral" refers for Hegel to that which proceeds from the interior of the will of the human subject, and by a relationship between the implicit will and volition, issues in morally free actual deeds. It can thus include moral wickedness which proceeds from the interior of the will. It is precisely because the moral will is inaccessible and so inviolable that it will be the measure of human action: "Human worth is estimated by reference to inward action and hence the standpoint of morality is that of freedom aware of itself."[40] The awareness of subjective will in morality is parallel to the awareness of external objects in the field of abstract right. The superiority of the moral order over abstract right lies in the fact that the concept is internal to the one who conceives it, whereas right was not. Yet because at this stage there is only room for a relation to self, to the will, and no sense of a relation to the universal, the rational will as such, there is scope for a further move to the level of ethical life, where the truth of abstract right and moral autonomy come together into sociality. This is best expressed by Hegel in the PR:

The second sphere, morality, therefore throughout portrays the real aspect of the concept of freedom, and the movement of this sphere is as follows: the will, which at the start is aware only of its independence and which before it is mediated is only implicitly identical with the universal will or the principle of the will, is raised beyond its [explicit] difference from the universal will, beyond this situation in which it sinks deeper and deeper into itself, and is established as explicitly identical with the principle of the will. This process is accordingly the cultivation of the ground in which freedom is now set, i.e. subjectivity. What happens is that subjectivity, which is abstract at the start, i.e. distinct from the concept, becomes likened to it, and thereby the Idea acquires its genuine realization. The result is that the subjective will determines itself as objective too and so as truly concrete.[41]

With this identity of the good with the subjective will, we reach the stage of the ethical life, that stage in which we shall finally encounter the reality of the state. Since it is here that we meet the concrete, it is here for the first time that we shall discuss the aspects of human sociality, practices and institutions with which we are familiar, rather than, as in previous stages, be engaged with abstractions from those practices and institutions—right, wrong, good, evil, purpose, and so on. And as the truth of abstract right and morality, the matter considered under those categories is not now discounted or transcended, but both surpassed and incorporated, the true philosophical meaning of *aufgehoben*.

Sittlichkeit, usually translated as "the ethical life," is human sociality, consciously ordered:

When the onesidedness (of abstract right and morality) has been overcome, then subjective freedom exists as the universal rational will, in and for itself. The subjective freedom has its knowledge of itself and its way of thinking in the consciousness of the individual subject, while its activity and its unmediated universal actuality exists at the same time as custom. Here, self-conscious freedom has become nature.[42]

This universal actuality of *Sitte* occurs as "the spirit of a nation," or *Volksgeist*. The *Volksgeist* is "abstractly disrupted" into individuals, "of whose independence it is the inner power and necessity," and the individual subject "as an intelligent being, knows this substance to be its own essence."[43] In the *Philosophy of Right* the same point is made without the introduction of the notion of *Volksgeist. Sittlichkeit* is "the absolute will as what is objective, a circle of necessity whose moments are the ethical powers which regulate the life of individuals." This relation of parts and whole is one of interdependence: "To these powers individuals are related as accidents to substance, and it is in individuals that these powers are represented, have the shape of appearance, and become actualized."[44] As a result, the ethical substance as an object over against the subject is "an absolute authority and power infinitely more firmly established than the being of nature,"[45] but at the same time the spirit of the individual subject "bears witness to them as to its own essence," and "the subject is thus directly linked to the ethical order by a relation which is more like an identity than even the relation of faith or trust."[46]

> When individuals are simply identified with the actual order, ethical life (*das Sittliche*) appears as their general mode of conduct, i.e., as custom (*Sitte*), while the habitual practice of ethical living appears as a second nature which, put in the place of the initial, purely natural will, is the soul of custom permeating it through and through, the significance and actuality of its existence. It is Geist living and present as a world, and the substance of Geist thus exists now for the first time as Geist.[47]

But even here, Hegel concludes that the ethical substance, since it is the union of independent self-consciousness and its concept, "is the actual mind of a family and a nation."[48]

The three sub-sections of the discussion of the ethical life are the same in both the *Philosophy of Right* and the *Philosophy of Geist*—family, civil society, and state. There is always a temptation to read them as if the first gives way to the second, and the second to the third, in chronological progression. But to be true to Hegel's scheme it would be fairer to describe the first two as the components (moments) of the union that occurs in the third stage. They both represent partial truths of the ethical life, and it is the partiality which moves the one towards its opposite. So, the family is a natural bond pointing to the fact that the substantial existence of the individual is in its kind (*Gattung*). Because it is a natural association, there is no question of right:

> The family, as the immediate substantiality of Geist, is specifically characterized by love, which is Geist's feeling of its own unity. Hence in a family, one's frame of mind is to have self-consciousness of one's own individuality within this unity as the absolute essence of oneself, with the result that one is in it not as an independent person but as a member.[49]

Yet there is an ethical dimension to certain moments of the family: marriage, which is the formation of a new substantial unity; the community of the family as a moral person, in relation to its property, industry, and so on; and the realization of the ethical principle in educating children to independence, which is their "second or spiritual birth." Normally in the family, right has no more meaning than that of the individual's life within the family; in other words, a child is not given its rights in being brought up in a family, it is simply naturally assumed that the whole family is one unit of rights, and has its interior life accordingly. But the form of right comes to the surface when that right is threatened (a child's rights are in question as rights only when they are under threat, by abuse, for example), or when the family begins to dissolve. Hegel points out that when children begin to move away from the family, as they assert their independence and self-subsistence, "they now receive their share separately and so only in an external fashion by way of money, food, education expenses, and the like."[50]

Family decays *naturally*, in the mortality of its members, but also *essentially*; i.e., with the growth to self-subsistence of its members, they establish their personality as separate (symbolized, interestingly, in the acquisition of the right to property, which we have already seen is the key to independent personality in Hegel's anthropology).[51] With the introduction into the family for the first time of legal regulation, an element foreign to the family as such, yet arrived at naturally by the development of the internal essence of family, we approach civil society, the negative pole of ethical life, or the "world of ethical appearance."

As Hegel describes it, the family "disintegrates . . . into a plurality

of families."[52] It is easier to grasp the meaning here if we remember that "family" is an abstraction from the reality of human history. There are families, certainly, but the natural bond is not sufficient, and each individual family is itself constantly moving towards dissolution. That towards which they move is civil society, "the stage of difference." Alternatively, we can see the family as the abstract concept, the universal. The essential and natural disintegration of the family is the dialectical shift to the stage of difference, in which all the moments of the family are externalized or objectified, but in this process they seem to lose their association with the universal. This reflection into objectivity is "the disappearance of ethical life, or, since this life as the essence necessarily shows itself, this relation constitutes the world of ethical appearance — civil society."[53] The separation from the ethical is only illusory or a "pure mistake," since "while I suppose that I am adhering to the particular, the universal and the necessity of the link between particulars remains the primary and essential thing."[54]

The substance which is particularized into many persons at this stage, produces a world of individuals who do not share the natural bond of the family. Each concrete person is "a totality of wants and a mixture of caprice and physical necessity,"[55] but essentially related to other particular persons, similarly motivated and constituted. This leads to a completely interdependent system in which individual happiness and needs are actualized and secured: "This system may be *prima facie* regarded as the external state, the state based on need, the state as the understanding envisages it."[56] The ethical idea is at this stage lost, because it is present only as "the inner necessity behind this outward appearance."[57] The discussion of civil society exhibits the stages by which the principle of particularity becomes self-destructive, and the constituent individuals see the need for their collectivity to rest in something higher. This "something higher" is the union of the natural bond of the family with the system of interrelations of civil society, in essence the concept of the state, or the actualization of the ethical substance.

Looking a little more closely at civil society, it is striking how comprehensively Hegel's theoretical intent and practical commentary are linked together. We are now concerned with the world of human sociality. We have moved away from the abstraction of the nuclear family to look at the "state as the understanding envisages it," which is to say that the object of our investigation is the everyday world. If this everyday world is going to demonstrate its own unsatisfactoriness and its need to be grounded in some higher principle, then it must do it in ways which are evident to the investigator. And since the ways of civil society are sociopolitical processes, the ordinary methods of the science of political economy will be, for the moment, the tools of Hegelian analysis. Discussing political economy, Hegel says:

> Its development affords the interesting spectacle (as in Smith, Say and Ricardo) of though working upon the endless mass of details which confront it at the outset and extracting therefrom the simple principles of the thing, the Understanding effective in the thing and directing it. It is to find reconciliation here to discover in the sphere of needs this show of rationality lying in the thing and effective there. . . .[58]

Civil society sows the seeds of its own destruction, in its unchecked satisfaction of a never-ending flow of needs. Animals have needs, but these are limited in scope. The human transcendence of animal limitations is evident in the multiplication of real and imagined needs, and the ways of meeting them. In discussing needs, the subject of human being (*Mensch*) arises explicitly for the first time:

> In [abstract] right, what we had before us was the person; in the sphere of morality, the subject; in the family, the family-member; in civil society as a whole, the burger or bourgeois. Here at the standpoint of needs what we have before us is the composite idea which we call *human being*. Thus this is the first time, and indeed properly the only time, to speak of human being in this sense.[59]

Human needs exist as liberated from the natural necessity of animals; that is to say, the "mental needs arising from ideas" represent human freedom from the strict demands of the necessities of nature, although of course those continue to impinge. This thought gives Hegel occasion to make an attack on the notion of the superiority of nature or the natural, a common Romantic illusion. The supposed freedom of the "state of nature,' he says, when needs were confined to simple necessities, is false because it is "the mental plunged into the natural," whereas "freedom itself is to be found only in the reflection of the mind into itself, in mind's distinction from nature, and in the reflex of mind in nature."[60] Increasing social complexity is accompanied by the multiplication and subdivision of needs, in Hegel's view, and also by an increase *ad infinitum* in dependence and want, a state of affairs which the needy person cannot overcome, since what is needed to overcome it is someone else's property, the embodiment of the other's free will.[61]

This process of the multiplication of needs is matched by the division of labour that occurs in work, which is "the means of acquiring and preparing the particularized means appropriate to our similarly particularized needs."[62] Hegel presents the matter at this point without negative comment. Certainly, he notes the narrowing down of skills and the dependence on mechanization, but what is important to him here is that this involves a corresponding increase in interdependence:

> When human beings are thus dependent on one another and reciprocally related to one another in their work and the satisfaction of their needs, subjective self-seeking turns into a contribution to the satisfaction of the needs of everyone else.[63]

Something which exists in the ethical life is there for a purpose, not there to be overthrown. Thus, subjective self-seeking through the interdependence created in the division of labour is a "dialectical advance," and if it does lead to the conditioning of resources on the grounds of capital and skill, both of which are arbitrarily parcelled out in their different ways, it is idle "to oppose to this . ... a demand for equality." The real is not abstract equality and what ought to be; rather, "human beings are made unequal by nature."[64]

Time and again in the Hegelian corpus, we see evidence of this apparent acquiescence in the status quo, this deference to the rationality of the actual, this seemingly irredeemable conservatism.[65] As Charles Taylor has pointed out,[66] this is a useful point of comparison between Hegel and Marx. Both were aware of the inherent self-destructiveness of bourgeois society, but where the latter wished to move to hasten its disappearance, Hegel saw it as an essential moment in objective Geist, and so also cancelled and preserved in the higher demands of the state.[67] The differentiation of function of the Hegelian society is a direct result of human beings' subordination to the actualization of

Geist; the production of a classless society on Marxist lines is the logical conclusion of making human beings the measure of all.

This subordination shows up most clearly in Hegel in his account of the class-structure of society. Class differentiation is a direct result, he thinks, of the complexification of the social structure, and individuals are fitted into one or other class according to their "needs, means, and types of work relative to these needs, modes of satisfaction and of theoretical and practical education."[68] Avineri puts the contrast with Marx particularly well:

> For Marx, classes are aggregates formed by types of social labour, linked together by the common relationship of their members to the means of production, seeking a political articulation for their socioeconomic interest. The class nature of political power is to Marx a sin against the state's presumed claim to express the universal as against the particularism and egotism of civil society. For Hegel, the institutionalization of class relationships into the political structure is the way through which the atomism of civil society becomes integrated into a comprehensive totality. The different classes represent to Hegel not only modes of production, but modes of consciousness which are relevant to a society differentiated in its structure according to the criteria of Hegel's general system.[69]

Hegel's differentiation into classes is unconvincing. In the first place, the classes are divided according to the concept: they are three, the substantial or immediate, the reflecting or formal, and the universal class. These correspond to the agricultural, business and civil servant classes. An obvious question relates to the place of the proletariat in the system, but the more general unease is the suspicion that the classes are there to serve the comprehensiveness of the system, rather than discovered in human experience, which would be truer to Hegel's avowed method. Thus, the agricultural class is supposed to exhibit a mode of subsistence "which owes comparatively little to reflection," and so which parallels Hegel's idea of the family, having "the substantial disposition of an ethical life which is immediate, resting on family relationship and trust."[70] The business class reflects the rationale of civil society, working "essentially on the mediation of one human being's needs and work with those of others."[71] Finally, the class of civil servants "has for its task the universal interests of the community."[72] The situation of individuals in one class or another seems to occur, according to Hegel, through a sort of "weak determinism":

> The question of the particular class to which an individual is to belong is one on which natural capacity, birth, and other circumstances have their influence, though the essential and final determining factors are subjective opinion and the individual's arbitrary will, which win in this sphere their right, their merit and their dignity. Hence what happens here by inner necessity occurs at the same time by the mediation of the arbitrary will, and to the conscious subject it has the shape of being the work of the subject's own will.[73]

It seems fairly clear that the role assigned to subjective opinion cannot mean that the individual can choose his or her social class. We have already been told by Hegel that capital and skill limit freedom of choice, and our own experience teaches us that in large measure, in the nineteenth century and for much of our own, if not so certainly today, mobility between classes is the exception rather than the rule. What Hegel seems to mean is something much closer to his understanding of freedom. Just as for Hegel freedom does not primarily mean freedom to choose this or that, but freedom to fulfill the essence of finite spirit, so here, choice of class is not so much a matter of choosing to be a peasant or a civil servant, but *choosing* to be what I am, the act of will by which I determine myself; I actualize myself. For the same reason, once the choice is made, it cannot be changed, but it is precisely because classes have to do with modes of consciousness, and not with modes of production alone, that such a conservative picture is presented:

> An individual is actualized in becoming something definite, i.e. something specifically particularized; this means restricting self exclusively to one of the particular spheres of need. In this class-system, the ethical frame of mind is therefore rectitude and *esprit de corps*, i.e. the disposition to make oneself a member of one of the moments of civil society by one's own act, through one's energy, industry and skill, to maintain oneself in this position, and to fend for oneself only through this process of mediating oneself with the universal, while in this way gaining recognition both in one's own eyes and in the eyes of others.[74]

We have seen how the human capacity to feel needs which are more than strictly physically necessary leads directly to the complexification of society in order to meet these needs, the division of labour and mechanization of means of production, and the association of society into groups or classes for the furtherance of this process. All this is part of the necessary self-development of the idea in history, as it is also a series of necessary stages in the growth of civil society and its *Aufhebung* in the state. But it is important to grasp that this *Aufhebung* does not involve the destruction of civil society, as civil society itself did not mean the end of the family. In the dialectic, the transformation of the one into a higher stage is its cancellation and preservation. This is matched in human history by two movements. The first, expressing the cancellation involved in *Aufhebung*, is that in which the truth of history is revealed in a series of progressive approximations to the truth, finally reached in the standpoint of speculative reason, which not only shows the truth, but knows that what it shows is the truth. And the other reveals the sense in which the earlier stages are preserved: they continue to exist in human history as component parts of the new reality.[75] So family, civil society and its various elements continue as moments in the ethical life, each expressing parts of its truth, even when the whole truth of the ethical life has become apparent in the state and the other moments, strictly speaking, have become redundant. At an earlier stage, abstract right and morality have been surpassed in the coming to be of the ethical life, although the ethical life could not be understood except in terms of its being their synthesis. Later, Hegel will want to say that there is a sense in which religion is surpassed by philosophy, while it will be equally true that religion will continue to exist.

In the final two subsections which deal with civil society, the Administration of Justice (*die Rechtspflege*), and Police and Corporation, the elements in the analysis which lead towards the dissolution of civil society and its transformation into state come to the fore. Ideally speaking, the civil society should simply give way to the state; in actuality, the *idea* of the state becomes paramount. That is to say, from this point on the measure of a society will be the degree of its actualization of the idea of the state. But it would be a mistake to think civil society will disappear.

This is nowhere more evident than in Hegel's treatment of poverty, which seems to his mind to be an ever-present and ineradicable factor in human society. *Police* for Hegel means public authority, the action of civil society as it accepts its role as universal family and protects the rights and duties of those it has wrenched from their natural families. It must, for example, wherever possible, provide public education,[76] and, taking up now again the earlier mention of poverty as the product of the system of needs,[77] it must try to protect those who either by caprice or external circumstances have been reduced to poverty:

> The poor still have the needs common to civil society, and yet since society has withdrawn from them the natural means of acquisition and broken the bond of the family—in the wider sense of the clan—their poverty leaves them more or less deprived of all the advantages of society, of the opportunity of acquiring skill or education of any kind, as well as of the administration of justice, the public health services, and often even of the consolations of religion and so forth.[78]

Warming to his task, Hegel points out that the unimpeded activity of civil society itself, with its divisions of labour and intensification of needs, leads to "the dependence and distress of the class tied to work of that sort."[79] The net result of all this is the creation of a rabble of paupers, a proletarian class of rebellious poor. Hegel does not call this group "a rabble" merely on account of their poverty, but only as and when that poverty has joined to it "a disposition of mind, an inner indignation against the rich, against society, against the government, etc."[80] Belonging to no class, the group cannot be incorporated. But if the poverty is to be alleviated, it should not be done either through public assistance or taxation of the wealthy, both of which would further erode the self-respect of the poor. And it cannot be done by creating work, since this is only to increase production levels, whereas "the evil consists precisely in an excess of production and in the lack of a proportionate number of consumers who are themselves producers." So, whereas Hegel seems to believe in an early version of welfare capitalism, he also finds the basis of society in self-respect, and thus can conclude by commending a policy adopted only in the most thoroughgoing capitalistic or uncaring societies. In Britain, he says,

> . . . the most direct measure against poverty . . . . has turned out to
> be to leave the poor to their fate and instruct them to beg in the
> streets. . . . It hence becomes apparent that despite an excess of
> wealth, civil society is not rich enough, that is its own resources are in-
> sufficient to check excessive poverty and the creation of a penurious
> rabble.[81]

This is really where he leaves the problem of poverty, as endemic to
society. Moreover, this poverty has created a group which cannot be
incorporated, which are "classless." One cannot help feeling that in
failing to give a status to this group, he leaves Marx with exactly the
revolutionary class he needed. They may play their part extrinsically,
by highlighting the economic unsatisfactoriness of civil society, but
they are not one of the classes (*Stände*), they cannot feel that they
have a place in the Hegelian state.

But if some elements tending to the dissolution of civil society are
undoubtedly negative and threatening, others are promising signs of
a sense of something higher. Chief among these is the corporation,
which provides for the business class what the agricultural class has in
virtue of its closeness to the natural bond of family life, and the class
of civil servants has through its conscious explicitation of the universal, namely, the appearance of ethical principles as a factor in its activity. Corporation is "the second ethical root of the state, the one
planted in civil society."[82] Knox presents two very complex notes on
corporation,[83] but in essence it is enough to see them as labour
organizations or craft unions, in which the members are associated in
virtue of particular skills, for the protection of their business interests
and for the education of new members:

> In short, its right is to come on the scene like a second family for its
> members, while civil society can only be an indeterminate sort of family
> because it comprises everyone and so is farther removed from in-
> dividuals and their special exigencies.[84]

The minor details are not important here. It is more important to
recognize that within civil society there is need for, and hence a movement towards, the continuance or reintroduction of the family principle; that, in other words, unchecked civil society is somehow un-

satisfactory to those whom it has ripped from their natural bond. The corporation is a shelter to the business class, in contrast to the mere external organization of police or public authority. And it goes beyond the natural rights of the family to the same rights, now rationalized and made actual, since, for Hegel, reflection arises in the city: "Town and country thus constitute the two moments, still ideal moments, whose true ground is the state, although it is from them that the state springs."[85] Now we can see that the state, which we have treated as something to be brought about, is in fact the ground of that which seems to be bringing it about. Or, to put it differently, it is now apparent that these seeming steps to the state are really component parts of the whole reality, the truth of which is the state:

> Since the state appears as a result in the advance of the philosophical concept through displaying itself as the true ground of the earlier phases, that show of mediation is now cancelled and the state has become directly present before us. Actually, therefore, that state as such is not so much the result as the beginning. It is within the state that the family is first developed into civil society, and it is the idea of the state itself which disrupts itself into these two moments. Through the development of civil society, the substance of the ethical life acquires its infinite form, which contains in itself these two moments: (1) infinite differentiation down to the inward experience of independent self-consciousness, and (2) the form of universality involved in education, the form of thought whereby Geist is objective and actual to itself as an organic totality in laws and institutions which are its will in terms of thought.[86]

For the remainder of this work, our concern is with the state. We have gone into such detail about the preliminary stages or component parts precisely because they are essential to understanding what Hegel means by the state. He is not discussing a political monolith, nor merely concerning himself with the details of political organization. Certainly he is interested in structural minutiae, but only insofar as they contribute to actualizing and supporting the idea of the state. They are important only when they help to bring about and support in existence an enabling structure for fully human life. The fully human life is a life lived in community; this is the truth which the discussion of the state is meant to reveal. The two aspects of political organization and natural bond of feeling must come together, if the fully human life is to be lived, because these two are the truth of the finite spirits who make up human reality. From the beginning of the analysis of abstract right, we have been concerned in one way or another with the question of intersubjectivity. Abstract right was treated as if it were the primary moment, whereas it would be truer to describe it as the *primal* moment of relations between human subjects. It remains a part of human existence in the state, jealously guarded by the same structure which logically implies the transcendence of right in the adherence to a larger whole.

We shall pursue our analysis of the state in three stages, stages which do not correspond especially closely to Hegel's own subdivisions of the matter. In the *Philosophy of Right* he gives by far the largest amount of space to the delineation of the political features of the state, which fill out its designation as a "self-dependent" organism. But even the state exists in an intersubjectivity with other states, and so in his second subdivision he turns to the question of international law. Finally he looks at the union of the two: not the individual instantiation of the idea in the first or the external relations of different instantiations in the second, but the truth of the universal idea as that which is above and binding upon individual states. *Volksgeist* gives way to *Weltgeist*.

Our path will be a different one. Before setting out on it, a brief survey of the details of the Hegelian state is necessary. Then I propose to return to the question of the place of the state in the Hegelian understanding of reality. In what sense is it really the highest actualization of Geist in history? Thirdly, we shall look at the state in terms of the individuals who comprise it, and ask what it is that the state fosters and protects. And finally, we need to investigate the state's own *Aufhebung* in *Weltgeist*.

Chapter II

THE STATE

W e shall begin this chapter by constructing a general picture of the Hegelian state. This is not easy, because there is nowhere in history to which we can point and say, "*There* is Hegel's state!" And at no point did Hegel attempt to do such a thing himself.[1] He was always concerned with the *idea* of the state, the state considered as something explicitly rational.[2] At the same time, he descends to considerable detail, in particular about the relations of legislature, crown and executive, and about the role of the Estates, and there is no doubt that he had a particular mental image of his state, even if it was not modelled on that of his time in Prussia, or elsewhere.

Even so, it has to be said that his understanding of the state was to some extent a product of his reflection on his own world, in which the biggest single event was the conflict between nascent French republicanism and the aging Holy Roman Empire — effectively German. Events had revealed, he felt, that the time was ripe for a revision of the German political structure, and in his early essay on "The German Constitution," he attempted to present his arguments.[3] Fundamentally, he argued for the principle of common universality which we have already discovered lies behind his later concept of the state. Germany at the time was divided into about three hundred sovereign states and not only did this make a nonsense of "Germany" as such, but each individual state was itself the scene of merely particular interests.

The fully-developed conception of the state as it appears in the *Philosophy of Right* is a constitutional monarchy, in which the crown plays its role in relation to those of the executive and the legislature.[4] The legislature itself is subject to three influences: monarchy, executive and Estates (*Stände*).[5] And the Estates, in their turn, mediate between the people, considered as an undifferentiated mass, and the government. This "mediation" was not a result of what we would take to be the normal patterns of representative democracy; "one person, one vote" was an outmoded idea to Hegel, and belonged to the time of small and simple political groupings, above all to Athenian democracy:

> The circles of association in civil society are already communities. To picture these communities as once more breaking up into a mere conglomeration of individuals as soon as they enter the field of politics, i.e., the field of the highest concrete universality, is *eo ipso* to hold civil and political life apart from one another and as it were to hang the latter in the air, because its basis could then only be the abstract individuality of caprice and opinion, and hence it would be grounded on chance and not on what is absolutely stable and justified.[6]

The organization of individuals into classes had its political issue in the differing roles of the different Estates in the life of the nation. Some members of the so-called "agricultural class" have a clear role in the political Estates, but this should not lead anyone to think that Hegel wanted a peasant government. Sections 305–7 of the *Philosophy of Right* makes it quite clear that he is referring to that segment of society which we would probably call the "landed aristocracy."

> The class in question is the one whose ethical life is natural, whose basis is family life, and so far as its livelihood is concerned, the possession of land. Its particular members obtain their position by birth.[7]

Its capital is thereby independent of commerce, and so of the search for profit. It stands outside the possibility of being influenced either by executive or mob, and the way in which its wealth is tied up in land and "primogeniture" makes it unlikely that it will be wilful or capricious.

Obviously, this looks like an argument for plutocracy, but it is not so simple as that. Firstly, we have to remember that Hegel is looking at political history up to and including his own time, seeking the rationale for what had actually occurred. It would not be totally unfair to see that as searching out justification for the political *status quo* of a stable society. If, the argument would have to run, this society gives all human beings in it their essential freedom (of self-determination), then it is operating on rational principles. But the important point about this Hegelian aristocracy is that it is not aristocratic government, but aristocratic representation in the Estates as a political link between people and government. When the Estates meet, the landed aristocracy are entitled to be present as of right, whereas those who attend as representatives of civil society, not of "family," are appointed as deputies by society "articulated into association, communities and corporations."[8] They are not to be voted for in a way we should call democratic, but by the organizations they will represent, although they are not tied to the interests of those they represent, but are directed towards the universal good.[9] Hegel goes on to argue for the division of the Estates into two houses, and then for the freedom of public opinion.[10]

It would be possible to go into considerable detail here, but I hope to show that it would be pointless, almost by definition. The more detailed the discussion gets, the further away we move from the idea as such, the closer we get to dwelling on the accidental form in which the idea is brought to expression in Hegel's time. His thinking is radically time-bound, by his own admission;[11] and if we went into his discussion of free speech, or freedom of the press, or the role of the Estates, we should find just how conservative this picture of political life would be *by our standards*.

I have already mentioned the division of the state into three sections of legislature, executive and crown. The rationale for this division, sensible enough though it may in itself be, is less than convincing: the legislature is "the power to determine and establish the universal," the executive is "the power to subsume single cases and spheres of particularity under the individual," and the crown is "the power of subjectivity, as the will with the power of ultimate decision."[12] Here, in other words, the powers of the state are clearly identified with the three moments of the dialectic. Hegel's belief that in his time the principle of subjectivity was best guarded by a monarch is, of course, no justification for saying that in all times and all places the constitutional monarchy is what is best. Hegel is not arrogant about the role of philosophy in relation to human history. It can only describe, and from this description tease out the rationale, the essence of what appears. For our time, Hegel would allow us to choose that political form which protected the element of subjectivity, and also might help us to articulate our criticism of those which did not. We might use his insights, for example, to suggest that the involvement of the American presidency in the legislature limits the presidency's ability to work as the power of subjectivity, although there is nothing as far as I can see to prevent replacing the constitutional monarchy with some form of presidency and still having a Hegelian state. Or, the constitutional monarchy in Britain might be criticised for not leaving enough power with the crown, so that Her Majesty's signature on acts of parliament is a pure formality. Thus, there would be a constitutional monarchy in a stable and relatively free society which still did not fit Hegel's picture.

If we look hard at Hegel to discover what his ideal really is, we are forced back, it seems to me, to a very idealistic vision, one that is not and even perhaps cannot be instantiated. Its definition is as *community* in some sense, and Hegel comes close to describing it without structures in *Philosophy of Right* §260:

> The state is the actuality of concrete freedom. But concrete freedom consists in this, that personal individuality and its particular interests not only achieve their complete development and gain explicit recognition for their right (as they do in the sphere of the family and civil society) but, for one thing, they also pass over of their own accord into the interest of the universal, and, for another thing, they know and will the universal; they even recognise it as their own substantive mind; they take it as their end and aim and are active in its pursuit. The result is that the universal does not prevail or achieve completion except along with particular interests and through the cooperation of particular knowing and willing; and individuals likewise do not live as private persons for their own ends alone, but in the very act of willing these they will the universal in the light of the universal, and their activity is consciously aimed at none but the universal end.[13]

Obviously, the "principle of modern states" has come closer to that pattern. Certain forms of state: despotism, pristine democracy of the Athenian variety, a slave society under an ochlocracy or aristocracy—would definitely contradict the Hegelian definition, and he rightly saw in his times those kinds of states being replaced by relatively enlightened, relatively liberty-loving societies. He could also argue, of course, that with his own picture of the state having been fully developed, the truth was finally available and there was *in principle* no reason why society could not now smoothly progress in its instantiation of concrete freedom. Whether or not future societies would be structured on his model was no concern of his, but to the extent that they conformed to the definition of freedom, it would not matter what their external organization was.

In this chapter, as we try to see more clearly the ramifications of the Hegelian state, we shall have to keep all that in mind. It seems to me that Hegel's recognition of the role of philosophy in relation to history, in the preface to the *Philosophy of Right*, frees us from a slavish following of the historical forms of Hegel's day. What we are concerned with is his theory of the state, and the underlying metaphysical principles. Estates and monarchs are not in themselves important; structures of concrete freedom are. Immersed in human history, we face civil society; what the Hegelian vision arms us with is a method for discerning the rationality at work within it. Like any other metaphysic, it is a matter of meaning in history. The three sections which now follow in this chapter examine the state in relation to the Hegelian system as a whole, in relation to its component individuals, and in relation to the larger framework of other states and the meaning of history as a whole.

Objective and Absolute Geist: How They Interconnect

In the *Encyclopaedia*, Hegel says that "the entire development of Geist . . . is the raising of itself to its truth," and this is a process of self-transformation, self-differentiation, "and the bringing back of its differences to the unity of its notion."[14] This is achieved by triumphing over sheer externality, reducing it to inwardness or "idealizing" it. Once again, the human pattern of coming to know something is illuminating: in overcoming the otherness of the other, knowing it as other and hence knowing myself as other (for it and for my knowledge of it), I bring the other under control of my mental processes (reduce it to a "moment"), and I become I. This human capacity for idealization is the exercise of *freedom*, and this notion of freedom is one important way to look at the essential unity of the three moments of the dialectic. The essence of Geist is freedom, but for Hegel freedom is self-relation, or total absence of dependence on the other. This is why the overcoming of the other in any act of knowledge, and its reduction to a moment, is itself an exercise of freedom, and so of the essence of finite spirit as a knowing agent. But freedom itself is total absence of dependence, total knowledge, the absolute Idea. Clearly, absolute Geist stands at the summit of this process, because absolute Geist is the point at which everything is reduced to a moment except Geist itself. The process, in a manner of speaking, has become the whole truth, or more correctly, has come to know itself as the truth. Hegel makes all this quite clear in the very important *Zusatz* to Enc. 382:

> The substance of Geist is freedom, that is, independence from an other, or self-relation. Geist is the concept which is for itself, having itself as an object. In the unity of the concept and objectivity present in Geist, reside its truth and its freedom. Truth makes spirit free, as Christ has said; and freedom makes it true. The freedom of Geist is not one merely of externality to the other, but rather an independence from the other achieved through it.[15]

It may not be coincidental that "Christ" is invoked somewhat unnecessarily at this point. The understanding of incarnation of especially Logos-theology is very close to Hegel's conception of freedom as self-relation. In Logos-theology, Christ is the "expressed word" of the Father; the image represents the way in which a thought, even a word, both leaves the speaker and yet remains part of the speaker at the same time. This self-alienation of the Father in the Son is exactly parallel to the self-othering involved in the act of thinking. As Quentin Lauer brings out so well in *Hegel's Concept of God*, thinking "is an acting involving no being-acted-upon." The thought is produced by the thinking subject, for Hegel. And this is as true for the finite as for the infinite subject. If absolute Geist is to be defined as infinite self-activity or thought, then finite being is finite Geist in virtue of sharing in that same "geistlich" activity of self-relation or freedom. Nor does finite Geist simply ape or parallel the activity of infinite Geist, but it truly participates in the same reality. It really is Geist, not least because the Hegelian infinite includes the finite, as we have already seen above.[16]

Now if the concept consists in the recognition that freedom, understood as self-relation, is the concept, then the divine/human process is the move from the self-relation itself, the concept in itself, freedom itself, or subjective Geist, to a knowledge *that it is free* as self-related, that this is the concept, or truth: to, in other words, absolute Geist. This process of coming to know is one of passing over into and overcoming, idealizing, externality. And the context in which this is achieved is human history. The state is at the summit of objective Geist precisely because in the realm of externality it is the structure of concrete freedom, and in it the same relation between individual and corporate freedom is expressed in externality as, in the process as a whole, is expressed between finite and absolute Geist. This dialectic of part and whole will be the subject of the next section, when we turn to the mechanics of the state.

If the concept is, in principle, truth, then the actualization of the concept involves the knowledge of the truth, and its externalization in the realms of nature and finite spirit is the path to the appropriation of truth. One of the most helpful means towards understanding Hegel's system is to see it as involving three principles, all three of which are so interrelated that any one can be seen as necessary to the existence and separateness of the other two. This is the theory of the so-called "triple syllogism," elaborated in great detail by Emil Fackenheim,[17] and from time to time emerging explicitly in Hegel's writings in one form or another. The three fundamental principles of the system are the logical Idea, nature and Geist; or, theoretical structure of reality, external reality, and comprehension of reality. The theoretical structure is a kind of logical hypothesis about the shape of external reality; external reality is that place, where, if anywhere, the truth of that logical structure will be apparent; and the comprehension of reality is that which will bring the two together. Obviously, then, Geist as that which seeks to demonstrate that the structure of external, non-rational nature accords with a rationally ordered concept, mediates the logical Idea to nature, and nature to the logical Idea. Similarly, Geist understands nature in terms of the logical Idea, the theoretical structure; otherwise it would face brute facticity—without the capacity for abstraction, that is to say, there could be no cognition. And so the logical Idea necessarily mediates between nature and Geist. Finally, the logical Idea is only true, only has actuality, if it is evident in the external world, and known to be evident. And so nature stands in a mediating position between abstract hypothesis and concrete actuality of the concept.

A similar threefold set of relationships is evident in Geist alone: we find subjective, objective and absolute Geist. The stage on which we find these three is, of course, the human world. Subjective Geist is the structure of the human being, just as the subjective moment of the dialectic as a whole is the structure of the concept. Objective Geist is the actual human world, in which rational human beings seek more or less successfully to structure their world rationally. Absolute Geist is the realm of activities through which finite Geist comes to a recognition that Geist is the truth of all that is, namely, art, religion and philosophy. Any one of these three principles or moments can be expressed as a mediator between the other two. All are equally necessary: without subjective Geist there would be no structure, without objectivity, no actuality, and without absolute Geist, no knowledge. The knowledge of Geist is the union of pattern and actuality. The pattern or structure is discerned in rational reflection on actuality. And the actuality of Geist is the externalization of a rational pattern.

The drama of human history does not itself follow a conscious pattern. The pattern (the rational discerned in what appears) is apparent in human reflection upon it, which occurs, in principle, in the viewpoint of the speculative philosopher, standing at the "end of history." So human history exhibits a welter of mixed motives, a chaos of human institutions, in which there is an underlying rationality. The process of the examination of objective Geist, in the *Philosophy of Right* in particular, is a painstaking systematization of the data of human history. History does not happen like that, and it does not progress in an orderly fashion to its summit in the state. To place the state at the high point of objective Geist, as Hegel does, is to say only that it is in the idea of the state, insofar as it is actualized, that Geist is to be found most pre-eminently present in the institutions of human history. It is "more" present even than in the activity and existence of the individual finite Geist, since the truth of Geist is uncovered more fully in the dialectic of part and whole:

> The state is the absolutely rational inasmuch as it is the actuality of the substantial will which it possesses in the particular self-consciousness once that consciousness has been raised to consciousness of its universality. This substantial unity is an absolute unmoved end in itself, in which freedom comes into its supreme right. On the other hand this final end has supreme right against the individual, whose supreme duty is to be a member of the state.[18]

And so, Hegel goes on in the *Zusatz* to the same paragraph, "the state is Geist objectified." It will become much clearer in the next section, when we discuss this dialectic of part and whole in more detail, and look at the reciprocity of the individual and the community, why this must be so. For the moment, let us leave it at saying that the state is the concrete universal, and the individuals which comprise it are the particulars. Hence their true freedom and actuality can only be expressed by fulfilling their nature, as it is expressed in the concrete universal. And the concrete universal itself expresses in history the abstract universal of subjective Geist.

The time has now come, however, to try to say what the difference between absolute and objective Geist truly is. We have so far said that absolute Geist is the comprehension and the comprehending unity of pattern and externalization. What it comprehends is the truth of what is, and the truth of self, and the truth that its own truth is the truth of what is. The question that must now be asked is this: why does truth reside fundamentally in the idealization, and not in history itself? Why is human history a moment in the process, and not the process a moment in human history? Behind this question lies the challenge to the concept of absolute Geist, thrown down by the "left-wing" Hegelians, above all by Feuerbach, and made the basis of the Marxist critique of Hegel. It is because ultimately I wish to defend the religious and theological significance of the philosophical cohesiveness and adequacy of the Hegelian vision as a whole, that the challenge will have to be faced sooner or later. The fashion, espoused even by intelligent and sensitive exponents of Hegel, such as Fackenheim and Taylor, of selective appropriation of Hegel's insights and total rejection of his central notion, calls forth the question: why, if it is extinct, is it so nourishing? Neither Fackenheim nor Taylor, so far as I am aware, is a Marxist or an atheist, but this selectivity about Hegel may partially be the inheritance of the Marxist critique, and is certainly partially due to the fact that Fackenheim's Judaism and Taylor's inadvertence to the Christian roots of the Hegelian vision deprive them of the cognitive lynch-pin of the entire argument, the historical fact of the Incarnation, as the root of the idea of incarnation.

The central issue in the left-wing critique of Hegel is as well expressed by George Rupp as by anyone.[19] Rupp points out that Feuerbach and Marx merely extend the criticism voiced by David Friedrich Strauss. Strauss's attack on christology was principally founded on opposition to building absolutes upon a particular historical figure. Moving the investigation from Jesus of Nazareth to the question of God, Feuerbach and Marx in their different ways are participating in the same repudiation "of commitments which are construed as transcending the experienced order of natural and human phenomena."[20] Hegel, on the other hand, has to be one of the principle exponents of the "scandal of particularity." For him, the event of Christ is the key to the pattern of universal reality.

There is another interesting point here. The two traditions which stem from Strauss on the one side, and Feuerbach and Marx on the other, are historicism and atheism. The failure to pursue historicism to its logical conclusion in atheism, the loss of nerve which can be traced without much difficulty in nineteenth and twentieth century thought, produced a flight into the privatization of religion and religious experience, whether into a classical pietism, or into some form of existentialism. Both erect images of God essentially foreign to historical process, the one to deny that God has any place other than the heavens, the other to deny that God belongs anywhere but in the human will. The Hegelian genius, of course, was to derive a metaphysical vision from a hypothesis uncovered in human history, which envisaged a God who was in and yet beyond, who overreached history and yet was validated by historical events. We shall have much more to say about this later; strictly philosophically, however, the two positions—those of Strauss, Feuerbach and Marx on one side, Hegel on the other—come down to the former group's denial, the latter's upholding, of the reality of absolute Geist.

In terms of objective Geist, the question can be phrased this way: is the state something greater than the individual, or is the individual the true meaning of the state?[21] It is here, in the politicization of the originally religious left-wing critique of Hegel, that Feuerbach is crucial, as Henning Ottmann has shown.[22] There is certainly a sense, which Karl Barth points out, in which Feuerbach neither denies God nor denies theology, although only the sense that the terms are retained while emptied of their specifically theistic orientation.[23] God's nature is reduced to the true nature of human beings, *materialistically understood*; this is not the same as saying that there are points of likeness or even unity between divine and human, which latter is at least an arguable theological position. Theology is reduced to anthropology; this is different from the claim that theology is christology, which has in train some anthropological significance. It is for this reason that Feuerbach's identification of the roots of the "theology is anthropology" perspective with Luther's turn to the question of God *quoad nos* is a basic misunderstanding of the Christian God.[24] "God out there" or "in self" is an empty formalism if it is not a concept arrived at from reflection on the effects or works of God. In this sense, theology is always talk about God "for us."

But Feuerbach's reduction leads him to say that politics must be put in the place of religion. Feuerbach found Hegel asserting the state in a way which denied the primacy of the human subject, and also fragmenting the one human being, according to what he was discussing, into person, or subject, or burger.[25] But interestingly, the inversion of Hegel's thought that constitutes Feuerbach's attitude, his determination to wrench it away from the question of religion to that of politics, is as much an argument for the essentially Christian roots of the Hegelian philosophy as anything Hegel himself said, or his right-wing interpreters later added. Feuerbach saw the essential unity of the metaphysical and the Christian impulses; history is given a meaning, and that meaning somehow transcends the history in which it is discovered by the historical agent of discovery, human being. The human being attributes meaning to history, and claims that it is not reducible to history itself.[26] In other words, human beings (not all, of course) see the comprehension of world-process as something more than the world-process itself. This is what Hegel is saying, in arguing the *Aufhebung* of objective into absolute Geist. And this is precisely why the overturning of the Hegelian vision is at once a religious and a political act. You have to choose: the primacy of thought over being, with Hegel, or the primacy of being over thought? Feuerbach has no doubts:

> The true relationship of thought to being is simply this: being is subject, thought predicate. Thought comes from being, and being does not come from thought.[27]

Marx was fairly scornful of the attitudes of the young Hegelians, and certainly did not exclude Feuerbach from criticism in his contention that:

> The old Hegelians had *comprehended* everything once they reduced it to a Hegelian logical category. The young Hegelians criticized everything by imputing religious conceptions to it or declaring everything to be theological. The young Hegelians are in agreement with the old Hegelians in believing in the governance of religion, concepts, a universal principle in the existing world. But one party attacks this governance as usurpation, while the other party praises it as legitimate.[28]

Marx's major direct criticism of Feuerbach, however, is that he is over-concerned with the abstract individuality of the human being, and does not advert to the appearance of the human essence in socialization.[29] In this respect, it would seem that Feuerbach has stepped back from the genuinely Hegelian position that the fullness of human being occurs in community. And, of course, as I hope we have already shown, the contention that the individual is submerged in the state is an "undialectical reduction" of the complexity of Hegel's views.

Marx did not come immediately to his belief that Feuerbach was in essence also working with abstractions. In formulating his major critique of Hegel, for example, he spoke respectfully of Feuerbach as "the only person who has a serious and critical relation to Hegel's dialectic."[30] He praised Feuerbach for the recognition that philosophy was "religion brought into thought," for founding genuine materialism, and for opposing the central Hegelian notion of the negation of the negation.[31]

This last is the true heart of Marx's own critique of Hegel's abstraction. Marx had a great deal of respect in particular for the *Phänomenologie des Geistes*[32] and above all for the fact that through the Hegelian dialectic of negativity, Hegel understood that human self-creation was a process, and so that labor was crucial to the overcoming of alienation. But unfortunately, although Hegel had the correct insight, it was merely formal, pure abstraction. This was because Hegel took the essence of human life to be self-consciousness, and hence alienation is not real alienation but the alienation of self-consciousness. By making consciousness paramount, objectivity becomes "only the phenomenal being of the alienation of real human life, of self-consciousness,"[33] whereas for Marx, truly human, natural being must be expressed in being as well as in thought. Because Hegel has made the abstraction true and prior to objectivity, the abstraction is for him true human life. But because he sees it as an abstraction, and so as an alienation of life, "it is regarded as a divine process and thus as the divine process of humankind; it is a process which man's abstract, pure absolute being, as distinguished from himself, traverses." The subject of the process itself, which "first emerges as a result," is "the subject knowing itself as absolute self-consciousness, is therefore God, absolute spirit, the self-knowing and self-manifesting idea." And so "real human being and real nature become mere predicates, symbols of this concealed unreal human being and unreal nature."[34]

The year in which Marx wrote the above, he also published an essay in the *Deutsch-Französischer Jahrbuch* which is famous above all for containing the first mention of his faith in the proletariat. But it also illustrates the connection between religion and philosophy once again. Religion is an illusory product of deficient self-consciousness, a "general theory" of the perverted world of the state and society. Religion is

the world's encyclopaedic compendium, its logic in a popular form, its spiritualistic *point d'honneur*, its enthusiasm, its moral sanction, its

solemn completion, its universal gound for consolation and justification. It is the fantastic realization of the human essence because the
human essence has no true reality.[35]

The flight to religion is the grounding of objectivity in something
other than objectivity, in abstraction. It is the claim that meaning
makes the human being, where the truth for Marx must be that the
human being makes meaning. It is to say that:

> To be a pear is not essential to the pear, that to be an apple is not
> essential to the apple; that what is essential to these things is not their
> real being, perceptible to the senses, but the essence that I have ex-
> tracted from them and then foisted on them, the essence of my
> idea—Fruit.[36]

The same criticism is operative in Marx's attitude to the Hegelian
state. State is an abstraction from the reality of civil society, and by
the application of this abstraction, the real human beings of the real
civil society are alienated from their real world. Civil society is taken
to be the falsity, state (abstract state) the reality. Even the contradictions of objective political life are only contradictions in the world of
externality, exisiting in unity in the abstract idea. But for Marx, if
contradictions are found in society, they are essential contradictions,
because this is the only essence there is. So, says Marx, Hegel

> does not want the actual universal, the political state, to be determined
> by civil society, but rather civil society to be determined by the
> state. . . . Hegel's chief mistake consists in the fact that he conceives
> of the contradiction in appearance as being a unity in essence, i.e., in
> the idea; whereas it certainly has something more profound in its
> essence, namely, an essential contradiction.[37]

And overall, in the *Philosophy of Right* and in the Hegelian system in
its entirety, "the important thing is that Hegel at all times makes the
idea the subject, and makes the proper and actual subject, like
political sentiment, the predicate. But the development proceeds at
all times on the side of the predicate."[38]

> Thus empirical actuality is admitted just as it is and is also said to be
> rational; but not rational because of its own reason, but because the

empirical fact in its empirical existence has a significance which is other than itself. The fact, which is the starting-point, is not conceived to be such but rather to be the mystical result. The actual become phenomenon, but the Idea has no other content than this phenomenon.[39]

Feuerbach, Marx and the young Hegelians in general were completely aware that the Hegelian system was, and was meant to be, a Christian philosophy. The move from Hegel to Marx involves the recognition that speculative philosophy is in all essentials the same as theology, and the further conviction that this theology and philosophy must be replaced by politics. It might be thought that Hegel was concerned with politics in the *Philosophy of Right*, but in fact he was merely extending the priority of thought over being to political life. When Marx concluded his theses on Feuerbach with the aphorism that came to be his epitaph—"Philosophers have only sought to interpret the world, but our purpose is to change it"—he was saying something with which Hegel could have no quarrel. After all, it was Hegel in the preface to the *Philosophy of Right* who declared that philosophy was a descriptive science which "came after," and that its role was in the recapitulation of the meaning of the contingent, the discernment of the rationality of the actual. For philosophy to seek to prophesy or to plan for the future was to step beyond its true role. If anyone said that philosophy was useless in improving the human lot, Hegel would say that they were right. And if anyone said that what was important in the world was change and not interpretation, well, they might be right, but they were not doing philosophy.

Nevertheless, this is obviously not the end of the story. If a philosophical system interprets the era of human history in which it stands, it does so in terms of certain fixed conceptions of human nature, of history, of human society, which may be relative to its time, but which as relative to its time at least implicitly project its understanding as true, and so presumably as in principle applicable to the future. Hegel may be a child of his time in proposing his complex dialectic, but he surely does not think that a new order of reality will hurry upon the stage as his coffin is wheeled off it. He is not so sure that his answers are definitive, despite many assumptions about the "closed" nature of his system, but his lack of assurance is on the principle that philosophy is descriptive of what is, not prophetic of what is to come. On the other hand, the Marxist or any other variety of revolutionary wisdom does not operate without equally fixed views of human nature, history, human society, and so on. It may indeed be dedicated to changing the world, and its politics may be the science of understanding which leads to practical proposals for change, but that political science has just as many philosophical presuppositions as speculative philosophy has hidden political implications.[40]

In a later chapter, I shall be presenting a view of Hegel's state as the context of a dynamic and unfolding struggle for a better world, funded by a religious vision on Hegelian lines. Like all such discussions, its roots will be an anthropological vision. (The difference between Marx and Hegel is itself reducible to a different understanding of human nature.) For the moment, we return to the question of the relation between objective and absolute Geist, which at a purely philosophical level is the very same issue. Objective Geist is in itself the presence of the rational principle in human history. Absolute Geist is the validation of this principle in the knowledge *that* it is expressed in human history. From the standpoint then of finite individuals, the capacity to think is in itself a distancing from the reality about which they are thinking, an at least theoretical othering of the everyday reality, so that the question of the meaning of reality may be asked. Hegel of course does not want to say that human beings do not think for themselves, but that in thinking they participate in a principle of rationality which goes beyond their thought processes, and which in theory at least has an existence independent of these thought processes, although its actuality is not separable from finite knowers. The autonomy of this principle of absolute Geist is evident as the truth of art, the truth of religion, and the truth of philosophy, all of which human activities in some way involve the principle in which the activity shares, but which it does not exhaust.

As we saw earlier in discussing the family, the civil society and the state, we have to avoid using the wrong model of the relationships. Hegel's treatment of subjective, objective and absolute Geist could lead the unwary to think of them as three stages which succeed one another in some chronological process. Yet they are all present (i.e., actual) only in the moment of actuality, which is the objective moment. In this mode of existence (the mode of the natural mediation, we might say), subjective Geist is actual as pattern, and absolute Geist as validation or comprehension. The absolute is the guarantee that what seems so, is so: it is the proof of the necessity of the contingent, for the contingent is a necessary moment in the absolute. In objective Geist, absolute Geist is present in its externality, as rationality, and promised in its fullness in its presence through representations (in art and religion). And since in itself absolute Geist is pure reason, thought thinking itself, the knowledge that it is so, which can only be known in a thought (that of speculative philosophy) is a true sharing in and a true presencing of the absolute Geist in human history. Human knowledge is the mode of the presence of meaning in human history.

It is my contention that the state is present in civil society, and has as much actuality, as absolute Geist is present in objective Geist, and has actuality there. The idea of the state is present in its externality wherever in the system of needs that is civil society there is a conformity to the true rational idea of the state; wherever, in other words, the conception of the freedom of the individual as a freedom together with other individuals in a perfectly free organism is adverted to and acted upon. Nowhere in his writings, as we have said before, does Hegel suggest that the perfect state has existed or exists in his time. The idea of the state is a rational ideal, in existence in greater or lesser actuality in different states in so far as they pursue the inherent rationality of human history. Yet it must also have representational force; it must be possible to image or imagine the true, full, rational state, the idea actualized in its fullness. I should like to suggest that the only possible image for the kind of state Hegel envisages is that of the "kingdom of freedom" or kingdom of God, and hence that the struggle for the actualization of the state, a struggle which philosophy documents, although it may have to leave it to politics to forward, *is* the struggle which is so frequently described as the struggle for the "coming of the kingdom." The tension between ideal and reality is not something which suggests that now we have a little of what we shall later have in full. On the contrary, world process can be promising (being as becoming) only if we possess the idea now in the mode of true reality (thought). As meaning in any present moment, this idea is the only way in which, through the contrast between fullness of meaning and paucity of actualization, history can carry itself forward politically (towards a politico-religious ideal) without the accusation that it is a speculative philosophical vision that is operating on an illusion.

The proof of the content of the last paragraph is the matter of the remainder of this work. I am thus not sidestepping the Marxist critique of Hegel by flying back into his own "abstractions." It is rather my contention that Marx's critique of Hegel is itself an abstraction if it fails to take into account the dynamic political significance of the philosophical vision. In other words, there is certainly a level of abstraction in the dialectical process, but if it issues, beyond philosophy yet in terms of the philosophical vision, in political action, then its criticism as abstract is itself an abstraction from the totality of the system, and, more importantly, from the human beings as the system understands them. Furthermore, and now going beyond Marx, precisely because of the dependence of the philosophy upon the incarnational principle of Christianity, that political dynamic is inseparable from a religious dynamic. Both grow out of the same vision of human beings as beings who precisely do not subject themselves to a self-projected principle of truth or meaning in which they have no share. So frequently in the interpretation of Christian thinkers, the wrong assumption is made about the meaning of God or the absolute. Atheists are perhaps not the best judges of the nuances of theism, and even a slight measure of naiveté can result in almost total misrepresentation. The Christian God is not only the totally other, but also the God who is real in a human being in history. It is through faith in and reflection on that human being that a Christian comes to see what God is like. Hegel follows this pattern, for it is from within objective Geist, where the incarnate Lord alone is encountered, that human beings move to the comprehension of Geist in its absoluteness (God), at the level of speculative philosophy.

The Ethical Substance: the Tension Between Individual and State

Some of what was said in the previous section could lead us to think of the state as somehow personified. Certainly, the Marxist accusation that human beings in Hegel's view have to submerge their autonomy in some rational monolith could give that impression. Yet the truth of the matter is that the state only has actuality in the relation between individuals and idea. There are a number of ways to express this; we can say, for example, that the state is the bond of love proper to the family, projected into a conscious universality in the world of civil society. More purely philosophically, we can describe it with Hegel as "the ethical mind *qua* the substantial will manifest and revealed to itself."[41] Or we can choose an expression in terms of freedom:

> The state is the actuality of concrete freedom. But concrete freedom consists in this, that personal individuality and its particular interests not only achieve their complete development . . . but . . . they also pass over of their own accord into the interest of the universal.[42]

The state has its immediate existence entirely impersonally, in custom (*Sitte*) and its mediated existence only in "individual self-consciousness, knowledge and activity." The fullest and clearest presentation of this interrelatedness of substance and subject occurs in section 258 of the *Philosophy of Right*:

> The state is the absolutely rational inasmuch as it is the actuality of the substantial will which it possesses in the particular self-consciousness once that consciousness has been raised to consciousness of its universality. This substantial unity is an absolute unmoved end in itself, in which freedom comes into its supreme right. On the other hand, this final end has supreme right against the individual, whose supreme duty is to be a member of the state.[43]

The state is the universal. It can be considered internally, in which case it exists as a whole in relation to the constituent parts, which Hegel calls "the extreme of individuality as the multitude of individuals."[44] Or it can be considered in terms of its relations externally (with other states, for example), in which case it is itself an individual.

In order to understand all this, we need to come back to the two key notions of rationality and freedom. We might express rationality as the consonance between the idea and its actuality. Thus, the state can be termed absolutely rational when and if the individuals through whom the truth of the state is mediated, mediate that truth in conscious reference to it. Absolute rationality is absolute Geist, the perfect actualization of the idea in and through the moment of individual finite spirits. Freedom in the Hegelian sense is not far from the same notion; it is defined in the *Philosophy of Right* in the context of the difference between nature and Geist. Nature exists in the form of externality; that is to say, it has no self-consciousness. But the individual finite Geist distinguishes itself from nature in virtue of its capacity for positing the other as other. The ability to abstract, to see the other as other, is freedom, because it is the power over content, and in the exercise of this power over content, the "absence of dependence on an Other," the relation of self to self is expressed: "It is through the other and by the triumph over it, that Geist comes to authenticate itself and to be in fact what it ought to be according to its concept."[45] This process is the way in which Geist creates its freedom, and objective Geist is the moment in which this is effected, since this is the moment of actuality. The freedom of Geist is effected through the free acts of the individual subjective wills.

> The entire development of the concept of Geist exhibits only Geist's freeing itself from all forms of its existence which do not express its concept.[46]

Thus freedom is the process of conforming to essence.

This freedom comes about in the transformation of the forms of existence which do not correspond to the notion of Geist into an actuality that does. The true development of the idea of freedom is brought into the domain of historical development, and in this moment of objective Geist, it has its actuality as the state. But the state is actual in history as "Geist objectified," and so it must not be confused with the various historical particularities which have to do with the formation or origin of states. In this relation between the idea of the state in history, and historically developed states, lies an important clue to the question of the relation of individual and community in Hegel's vision.

No state is or has been a perfect instantiation of the idea of the state. For it to be so, it would take a community of perfect individuals to accomplish it. Moreover, no state exists where civil society does not also exist. But the role of civil society is in relation to the self-interest of individuals, which is best met in some free association in a system of needs. The relation of the state to the individual is not a contingent one, however: it is the substantial unity of the freedom which is expressed in the individual subjective will. Its relation is to the essence of the individual, and hence it is a necessary relation. The individual lives and acts in an interdependent society, a system of needs, and thus is related by choice (in principle) to a civil society. The individual could always refuse to participate, or move to another civil society. But the relation of the individual to the state is a necessary relation, because this is reference to the truth of self, and only in this relation is the individual *in* truth, *in* freedom.[47] The rejection of this relation would be the descent to mere self-reference, existence in civil society alone, and would be a rejection of freedom and truth because a rejection of the nature of human being. And so:

> Since the state is Geist objectified, it is only as one of its members that the individual has objectivity, genuine individuality, and an ethical life. Unification pure and simple is the true content and aim of the individual, and the individual's destiny is the living of a universal life.[48]

Here we need to say a word or two about ethical action. Ethical activity for Hegel is any action which has as its result an increase in freedom, understood as lack of dependence on the other. Through the exercise of rationality and its capacity of abstraction, the individual masters experience by idealizing it. At the same time, the individual affirms his or her true essence as rational thought, and in this affirmation simultaneously actualizes the substantial will. Through free actions, the community of freedom is actualized. Through activity done in accordance with the true nature of human beings, the state is present in the world. And the idea of the state as the ethical substance is the idea of a community in which all actions are done in accordance with the truth of human nature, and thus a truly free, absolutely rational community is present in history. But this is only the idea, and although history, true history, is the actualization of this idea, its actuality in history is as the law or principle of the state, not as a concrete or objective reality: "So far as the authority of an existing state has anything to do with reasons, these reasons are culled from the forms of the law authoritative within it."[49]

Clearly, then, there is a sense in which a Hegelian ethic will be formal. There is nothing in the injunction to follow the true nature of human being as rational that can give any clue to the content of ethical decisions in specific circumstances. Yet Hegel believes that he has carried the Kantian moral autonomy beyond the point at which it is a mere *empty* formalism. Hegel admits that "the good is characterized to begin with only as the universal abstract essentiality of the will, i.e., as duty," and therefore that it should "be done for duty's sake."[50] But the Kantian view settles for the *moral* position, without moving to the level of ethics (*Sittlichkeit*), and this "is to reduce the gain to an empty formalism, and the science of morals to the preaching of duty for duty's sake."[51] Charles Taylor carries this argument forward very clearly.[52] Taylor sees Hegel as having overcome the formalism of the Kantian autonomy of human freedom by its replacement with human involvement in the freedom of Geist. The Kantian radical freedom renounces the determination of the will by any particular desire whatsoever, and so there seems to be no ground of action remaining:

> But everything changes if the will whose autonomy men must realize is not that of man alone but of Geist. Its content is the Idea which produces a differentiated world out of itself. So that there is no longer lacking the determining grounds of action.[53]

It might reasonably be thought, however, that the Hegelian Geist is no less abstract itself; it has for its essential content what look like the purely formal characteristics of unity, dividedness, and reunification. But as Taylor points out, and as we have already seen earlier, these apparently formal structures are "made the ground for the essential articulation of the state into estates and into levels of society."[54]

Hegel's appeal for the dimension of *Sittlichkeit*, as against the mere morality of the Kantian position, rests on the belief that human being is bound by its rationality to participation in a larger life than that of serving self. As we saw above, the relation of the individual to the state is a necessary relation, and this is the relation in question in *Sittlichkeit*. Again, Taylor draws attention to the root of the word in

Sitten or "customs." Because what we are enjoined to in the ethical
life is obligation to an existing community of which we are already a
part, with its already existing customs, so the obligation is to what
already is, and hence "there is no gap between what ought to be and
what is."[55] We should then avoid the impression that Hegel contrasts
morality and the ethical life; rather, he wants to place the former in
the context of the latter, because individual decision-making always
takes place in the context of a community and its customs. Taylor
presents Hegel's argument for the primacy of the state in three propositions "put in ascending order of contestability":

> First, that what is most important for man can only be attained in rela-
> tion to the public life of a community, not in the private self-definition
> of the alienated individual. Second, this community must not be a
> merely partial one, e.g., a conventicle or private association, whose life
> is conditioned, controlled and limited by a larger society. It must be
> coterminous with the minimum self-sufficient human reality, the
> state. . . . Thirdly the public life of the state has this crucial impor-
> tance for men because the norms and ideas it expresses are not just
> human inventions. On the contrary, the state expresses the Idea, the
> ontological structure of things.[56]

The first two of these propositions are correctly identified by Taylor as
relatively uncontroversial, and relate to the concept of Volksgeist or
"spirit of the nation." The third suggests that human being "is the
vehicle of cosmic spirit" and "that the state expresses the underlying
formula of necessity by which this spirit posits the world." Taylor does
not dismiss this, and he is right to place it third in ascending order of
difficulty, particularly in a system which claims to be moved by rationality. "There is only," says Taylor, "a very difficult doctrine of a
cosmic subject whose vehicle is man."[57]

Taylor's two works on Hegel are outstandingly clear interpretations
and expositions of his subject. They avoid extremes, they do justice to
the complexity of the subject-matter, and they are written in an ur-
bane and illuminating spirit. At the same time, they illustrate quite
clearly why it is so difficult for Hegel to be received with equanimity
in the modern age. Hegel's work is a Christian philosophy, and if the
Incarnation is not seen, as Hegel saw it, as *the* validation of what
would otherwise be a mere hypothesis about the structure of the

world-process, then the crucial points of the system can never convince. Like the Marxist, the contemporary rationalist or the thinker who is underschooled in the sophistication of incarnational theology will consistently fail to see the point, or will glide over it in an embarrassed semi-silence. Taylor is closer to the latter, although his exposition of the Incarnation is characteristically clear and helpful.[58] But when he comes to write his conclusions, Taylor is faced with the question, why Hegel's central thesis is dead, while his philosophy remains relevant today in a variety of ways. His answer is thorough and intelligent: Hegel sought to unite "the rational, self-legislating freedom of the Kantian subject with the expressive unity within man and nature for which the age longed."[59] But contemporary society built into itself the Enlightenment conception of human being as "a self-defining subject with an objectifying stance towards nature and social life." And Hegel's ontology could not cope with this, because he believed that human beings would come to see their true selves reflected in the social structures by which the idea was realized in history. Certainly, the twentieth century has not seen the renewal of *Sittlichkeit* that would probably have been a part of Hegel's vision, had he looked so far ahead. But neither has Hegel been utilized by the modern heirs of the Romantic or expressivist protest against technological civilization. And this, according to Taylor, is because Hegel is not only inimical to the Enlightment view, but also opposed to expressivism to the extent that his vision is one of the reconciliation of world and spirit, not of an opposition between the individual and society.

All this is clear and perceptive, but incomplete, because the fact of the Christian associations of Hegelian thought, and the demise of conscious Christian association in the philosophical world of the twentieth century, is not adverted to. If the expressivist protest against modern technological civilization is not entirely in cloud-cuckoo-land, then in principle it ought at least to be prepared to investigate Hegel as a means of support. But if it cannot or does not share his Christian presuppositions, then Hegel must seem incomprehensible, or at least fanciful speculation. Without an understanding and sympathy for the doctrine of the Incarnation, the Hegelian view cannot ultimately convince, and therefore cannot command assent. But if this is the case, then it may not be fair or correct to decide that the system is dead, though its usefulness lives on. Could it not be that it is ignored rather than dead? To misuse Chesterton, might it not be that rather than tried and found wanting, it has not been wanted, and therefore not tried? Twentieth century philosophy has shown a deep antagonism towards metaphysics, and the rejection of Hegelianism is one aspect of this attitude. The suspicion of metaphysics and the decline of conscious religious affiliation have occurred over the same time-span and are obviously related. This leaves us with a double-edged problem: on the one hand, it is not clear that something is dead simply because it is rejected, nor indeed that the Hegelian view of things is or need be universally rejected. On the other hand, we cannot expect to restore Hegelianism through a convincing apologia for incarnational Christianity. Yet Hegel would not, I suppose, wish to argue that his vision is only true as a result of Christianity; rather, that the Incarnation in the Christian sense is the revelation of the truth of the relation of absolute Geist and human being. It is not incarnation that accounts for the consistency of the philosophical vision with the facts of experience, but it is in the Incarnation, *ordo essendi*, that the trope by which experience can be interpreted is manifest.

It would seem, then, that Hegel's vision ought to be as useful as it is consistent for the contemporary non-Christian philosopher. As a Christian philosophy, however, its seriousness is in direct relation to its linkage with the central Christian doctrine of the Incarnation, broadly according to the understanding of the council of Chalcedon. For this reason, it is as alive as the doctrine of the Incarnation, and that doctrine in its turn is only dead if Christianity is itself dead. No doubt, many philosophers would wish to say that that should be the case, but it refuses to lie down and accept its philosophical fate. In the next chapter we shall be turning more thoroughly to this issue, but before we do so, we have one more line of approach to the Hegelian state to consider. We must look at the external characteristics of the state, and its relations to other states and to *Weltgeist*.

State and History

So far, we have investigated only the internal structure of the state, the sense in which it represents the universal over against "the extreme of individuality of the multitude of individuals." But there is also the matter of its identity and nature as a whole, and this can only be established in relation to other states, for "individuality is awareness of one's existence as a unit in sharp distinction from others."[60] In just the way that the human individual comes to be conscious of self through becoming conscious of the other, so the state recognizes itself as a unit, is able to define itself as having a shape and parameters, only in the recognition of other states. The relations between states, as between individuals, are handled through contract, treaty and custom.[61] The parallel with human individuals goes still further; just as society shows the evidence of the spirit of reason, despite the selfishness and caprice that infects the world of the system of needs, so the development of nations and the relations between them is a chaos of private interests and particularities, a dialectic of the *Volksgeister*, out of which arises the *Weltgeist*, "free from all restrictions, producing itself as that which exercises its right . . . over these finite minds."[62]

The point of all this becomes much clearer in the first of Hegel's lectures on the philosophy of history.[63] The *Philosophy of Right* (§§341–360) summarizes the course of the whole of the lectures, but hardly mentions the very helpful notion of providence; we are told that Geist exists in various forms in different cultural phenomena—in art, it is present as intuition and imagery, in religion as representation, and in philosophy as "pure freedom of thought." But it is also present in world history, as "the necessary development out of the concept of mind's freedom alone, of the moments of reason and so of the self-consciousness and freedom of mind."[64] While states, nations and individuals look to their own interests, "they are all the time the unconscious tools and organs of the *Weltgeist* at work within them."[65] Here we encounter the notion of "the cunning of reason," the idea that the actualization of Geist comes about inexorably in and through the particularities of history. And with this, we see for the first time the relations between the logical and chronological dialectic. In our discussions of *Recht*, *Moralität* and *Sittlichkeit*, and of the relations of family, civil society and state within the last category, we have been engaged in a process of structural dissection and rememberment, the better to understand the interconnections. But with each progressive stage, we also have seen that the prior stages existed not so much chronologically prior, but as structural moments at a more rudimentary or primary level than the higher stage at which we have been looking. In moving beyond state as a self-sufficient principle, to the way in which state itself is subordinated to the actualization of Geist in the world, there is no higher or more perfect subject to which to point. State is the perfection of the actualization of Geist in the realm of objectivity. Instead, we look to the perfection of the notion of state in a chronological progression. The *Volksgeister* are in their own era paramount, but engage themselves in an internal dialectic which leads to their passing over into something higher, not in the logical order, but in the historical process. One state succeeds another as a world-historical state, one era succeeds another, as through the succession Geist seeks to come to the perfection of actuality. The *Volksgeister* serve, then, individually, the higher expression of the truth of history, *Weltgeist*.

Let us look at the way the matter is dealt with in the lectures on the philosophy of history. Hegel begins by declaring his philosophical presupposition that reason "is the sovereign of the world," and therefore that world history will show itself to be a rational process. Accordingly, the philosophy of history is the rational consideration of a rational object. *Philosophical* history "means nothing but the thoughtful consideration of it."[66] The circularity is admitted as the inevitable presupposition of the historian; the result of the investigation has to be presupposed at the outset, and "whoever looks on the world rationally, sees it as rational."[67]

Hegel sees the conviction of the rule of reason in the world as evident in the beliefs that nature acts according to fixed laws (although they are mistakenly assumed to be externally imposed rather than immanent in nature), and that providence rules the world. The latter is a defective notion, he thinks, insofar as it depends on a hidden plan of providence, evident only occasionally in special acts of divine intervention, which are labelled "providential." For Hegel, this would be to ignore the scriptural truth that the Spirit leads into all truth, and the limitation of providence to natural events and isolated occurrences is to weaken the power of God. There is no reason why universal history cannot also be the realm of God's providence. God's revelation in Christianity is an expression of the divine desire that human beings should know God, and this knowledge thus becomes a duty. The knowledge of Gods' providence working in universal history is the philosophical consideration of the world process:

> The development of thinking Geist, which starts from a basis in the revelation of the divine essence, must finally come to the point where what was first presented to feeling and imagination is grasped in thought.[68]

In the philosophy of history, of course, it is not sufficient to appeal to the religious truth of providential care; the *science* of the philosophy of history exists to show that that religious truth is in conformity with the facts. In other words, the thoughtful consideration of history reveals just such a design.

Before he turns to history, Hegel establishes the abstract characteristic of Geist which is, as we have already seen elsewhere, freedom. Geist is self-contained existence with freedom as its essence, and this self-contained existence is self-consciousness. In self-consciousness, Geist distinguishes *that* it knows from *what* it knows, and thus comes to know itself:

> It is the judgment of its own nature, the activity of coming to itself, and so of producing itself, of making itself that which it is implicitly.[69]

Following upon this abstract definition of self-consciousness and freedom, universal history can be said to be the field in which Geist works out the move from what it is potentially to what it is in actuality. World history is the process of the self-actualization of Geist. Thus the final cause, the "end" of history in that sense, is Geist's consciousness of its own freedom, and in the same moment the reality of that freedom. This is the course of events charted by the lectures on the philosophy of history.

How, then, does Geist achieve this step from potentiality to actuality? Here we have to recall that the only way in which Geist is actualized in history is in the actions of individual finite spirits. Thus, the abstract destiny of Geist cannot be brought to actualization any other way than through the actions which result from the will of human beings. So, "without passion, nothing great has been accomplished in the world."[70] We return here once again to the cunning of reason; the abstract truth can be brought to full realization only through the objective realm in which the activity of human subjects is the only activity there is. Moreover, the cunning of reason is that it is not subject to the process of contending particularities and negation, but it leaves that role to passion, or, more precisely, to human interaction in history, and principally to the actions of those human individuals who turn out in some way to incarnate the spirit of their times, and thus to shift history significantly forward. These are the so-called "world-historical individuals," simultaneously agents and victims, who play their part on the stage and then disappear.

But there is a further and more exalted role for human beings in history, insofar as they are conscious of the ideal aim, which as a matter of fact occurs in religious or ethical activity, forms of activity "intimately connected with Reason." In ethical activity, the essential itself is the object of human existence, and since reference to the essential is found when the individual subjective will unites with the rational, substantial will (the ethical substance), we find the place of human freedom to be the state:

> This essential being is itself the union of the subjective and rational wills: it is the ethical whole — the state, which is the actuality in which the individual possesses and enjoys freedom, but in which that freedom is the knowledge, belief and will of the whole.[71]

Traditionally, the assumption has been made that by nature, human beings are free, and that their association in political or social groupings constitutes a voluntary limitation of freedom for the sake of some greater good. This view is directly contrary to Hegel's; all that the state limits, he believes, are the more brutish emotions and instincts, and in return it provides an objective basis for the freedom of human beings to express their true nature as rational, and as agents of the self-actualization of Geist, as constitutive moments in the process. And so the state is "the divine idea as it exists in the world."[72]

The major addition to our understanding furnished by the lectures is contained in the sections following the introduction. Here, Hegel seeks to demonstrate how Geist is manifest in chronologically successive eras and states — in the oriental, the Greek, the Roman and the Germanic civilizations. Each stage in history is that of a given *Volk*, and the *Volksgeist* of the particular *Volk* represents for that time the actualization in some way of Geist in general.

As usual, we must look for two principles expressed in two stages, and their unity in a succeeding third. The first is discovered in the "parochial" (Taylor's term) Greek god, and the consequently parochial *polis*. The linkage of the divine with the city gave the people a perfect image in which to recognize their political unity as free subjects. This free association in a whole is one element of the Hegelian state. The Athenian ideal was one form of *Sittlichkeit*, but restricted and therefore doomed to downfall, in the restriction placed on the extent of freedom. Only the "few" were free; Athens was a slave society, and so their conception of the state was not based on universal reason.

The second principle is provided by Roman society, the civilization which emphasized abstract right. The rights of the Roman citizen had nothing to do with a political role, coexisting as they did with the political form of empire. The person as the bearer of abstract right stands over against a political whole (universal) with which reconciliation is impossible. Something has been lost from the Athenian ideal, but something has also been gained. In this negative mode, the need for the ideal expressed in Athens is felt, but it is an ideal to which a return cannot be made. Instead, the unity is achieved in mediated form through Christianity, where the individual finite human being and the absolute are united once in Christ. This unity, realized now in principle, establishes the agenda for history, the full realization of the unity under the control of the Germanic peoples. The two means for this are the growth of the political essentials over the centuries—to Hegel, Estates, monarch and so on—and the concurrent spiritualization of the Christian reality, above all in the Protestant Reformation and the Enlightenment.

The Enlightenment itself, however, went too far in its assessment of reason, the centre of human freedom, as a purely human reason. The absolute freedom which was the implication of the general will theory of ethics which grew out of the Enlightenment, revealed its full horror in the French Revolution. Stuck in its negative moment, it was solely destructive, but in the effect it had on the minds of human beings, namely, terror, it turned them back to the universal. With Napoleon's conquest of Europe, the new state was born.

In our consideration of the state, we have finally been brought to the question of meaning in history. The notion of the state as we have tried to lay it out in the preceding sections is one of considerable logical coherence. It is that of the political constitution and customs of a given people, to the extent that these ways of being step beyond a system of needs and their servicing, a simply socio-economic unit, to the idea of a community in which the individual good and freedom is expressed and preserved in the common good and freedom. This "state," wherever and whenever it exists, is an expression of divine truth or Geist, because this pattern represents at the level of objective Geist the pattern of the relationship between divine idea, nature and Geist in the dialectic considered as a whole. It is therefore rightly to be declared to be the objectivation or "actualization" of Geist in history.

However, we also know that this state exists nowhere perfectly instantiated in the historical process. On the one hand, the various details of the constitutional and political make-up of the state as Hegel expresses them have never been reproduced in a historical state. On the other hand, the presence of the perfect state would produce a perfect society peopled by perfect human beings, and history would presumably have nowhere to go. Now, all that this might imply for Hegel as we have thus far expressed it, is that the perfect state has not yet appeared. History demonstrates the struggle towards the perfect state, and we are growing closer to its realization, with the contemporary constitutional monarchy of nineteenth century Prussia. But there are a number of reasons why this reading has to be rejected.

The preface to the *Philosophy of Right* contains Hegel's clearest statement of the limitations of philosophy. He leaves no doubt that for him philosophy describes what already is; it does not predict the future. He is quite clear that it comes upon the scene to describe what has occurred in the historical era at the end of which it stands, and he is adamant that like everything else it is "the child of its own times." For Hegel, then, philosophy is a historically relative expression of the truths held in the consciousness of the times in which it exists. At the same time, the whole drift of his system is that *his* philosophy is *the* speculative philosophy, and that it does describe the nature of reality. The speculative transformation of the truth represented in the Christian religion in its Protestant form brings about the full manifestation of world reality. Now we know how the whole thing works and what it is for. The problem of the reconciliation of these two elements—the logical direction of the system and the expressly conditioned nature of philosophical reflection—is *the* problem of Hegelian interpretation. It can also be represented as the question of the relation of the logical and chronological dialectics. The former is the problem addressed in the whole of the *Encyclopaedia*, the latter is its demonstration in history. Side by side, they represent the issue of meaning in history.

So we cannot ask Hegel to agree that his outline of the state has the status of an ideal which is growing slowly in the human consciousness, and destined one day to be incarnated in some particular historical community. This would be to ask him to go beyond the role of philosophy. Moreover, and more importantly, it would be to misunderstand the origin of the notion of the state. Hegel claims to found his philosophy in experience. It is the fruit of reflection on experience. Thus, the dialectical nature of his system is dictated not by some *a priori* consideration but by the simple observation that the nature of reality itself is dialectical. His philosophy is descriptive,[73] and therefore what he knows about the logical dialectic is, so to speak, derived from the careful investigation of history. The introduction to the lectures on the philosophy of history presents a hypothesis to be tested by the examination of history itself. The circularity of the Hegelian system is entirely consistent: obviously, if Geist moves through the moment of objectivity to its full self-realization, then the truth which is apparent in history is the moment of the actualization of Geist in the objective realm. History is the self-externalization of meaning, then, but this has to take place under the conditions of history. It has to come about through the role of human passions, mixed motivations, individual and national caprice, and so on.

In our discussion of the Marxist attitude to Hegel, we mentioned the primacy of thought over being as the Hegelian order of priority. It is a logical conclusion from this primacy of thought that the idea and its actualization is reality. Mere appearance which is not the actualization of the idea is a negative force; thus, for Hegel, evil is an absence of truth. Certainly, Geist can be described as the thought thinking itself, and human history is the externalization of this self-thinking thought. If the presence of meaning in history is coterminous with the actualization of Geist in history, then we can say that history exists to be the place in which Geist is actualized, that history exists for the revelation of meaning. History, if it is history, if it follows its purpose, is meaningful, which is only to say that in the show of events, the rational can be discerned. History is false to itself as human history if that rationality is obscured.

The role of history, then, is the revelation of meaning, and in a system in which thought has primacy over being, the revelation of meaning will occur not where it is incarnated in its perfection, but where it is thought in its exactness, and known to be so thought. This is the reason why Hegel can admit to the historical relativity of philosophical systems, but proclaim that with speculative philosophy the end of history is achieved. If Geist is self-thinking thought, and if finite spirits are moments in the process of Geist thinking itself, then with the thought of the speculative philosopher having come to see the truth of things, the true thought, the speculative parousia, has been achieved. When the perfect thought is thought, thought is perfect. When the truth of history can be understood and expressed, history is true. Where the idea of the state can be discerned within the workings of finite reality, the perfection of the state can be thought, and the state is therefore (in thought, and thus in actuality) perfect.

Chapter III

RELIGION

Writings on Hegel's understanding of religion are numerous.[1] In a single chapter within a larger work, I can hope neither to emulate their depth, not to summarize adequately the range of their perspectives. Several of these works attempt an overall view of Hegel's attitude to religion,[2] and others seek to interpret the system in terms of religion.[3] Further works concentrate on christology,[4] and on the *Theologische Jugendschriften*.[5] Although none of them are attempting quite what I shall try to do in this chapter, I am obviously indebted to some rather than others — in particular to Yerkes, Lauer, Theunissen, Fackenheim and Bruaire, and to Albert Chapelle for the excellent work in a volume of appendices on the comparative structure of the role of religion in the lectures on the philosophy of religion, the *Phenomenology*, and the *Encyclopaedia*.[6]

This chapter could divide into two very obvious halves: presentation of Hegel's views on religion, and a critical commentary on them. Since the treatment needs to be so compressed, however, I shall be alighting mainly on four topics. Firstly, we shall need briefly to see how Hegel envisages religion in general. Secondly, we need to look at the specific case of Christianity, or the absolute religion, and the identification between the dialectic of Geist and the economy of Christian salvation. Then, in third place, accepting the special role of Christianity in Hegel's vision, there is the question of the peculiar place of the state in the dialectic, and of how that looks when the dialectic is viewed in terms of Christianity. While treating this material, we shall constantly have to recall the shifting senses of the term religion—to give but one example, religion as the representational form of the dialectic, and religion as the institutionalized community within the social whole. This will lead us directly to the fourth and final heading of the chapter, where we shall have to uncover the primary sense of the word "religion," in Hegel, by asking the question: what is the role of Christianity in Hegel's world? I shall seek to show that its way of being within the social whole gives it a function very close to that of the state as we have seen it above, and thus that the way is open to asking the further question: is there a difference between the kingdom of freedom of Christianity, and the idea of the state? This will be the transition to the next chapter, where we shall face directly the question of the meaning of secularization.

What is Religion for Hegel?

We have seen in the earlier chapters how human history is the moment of Geist's objectivity, how Geist is present in the inherent rationality of human institutions, as well as in the process of knowledge of individual finite spirits. Religion is a further manifestation of human history; it will be expected, therefore, to have some expression in the institutions of objective Geist, and some reality in human reason. Religion exists within objective Geist. This must not be forgotten, even though we shall find ourselves talking of religion as a reference to *absolute* Geist. Religion has its whole being in objective Geist; if it didn't, then we should have to talk about God having a religion, which would be clearly absurd. What we can say about God, or Geist, is that God has or is pure self-consciousness, unmediated, passing through objectivity in order to come to a mediated self-consciousness. This is the form of expression of the process of the dialectic which we can associate more properly with the *Phenomenology*. The progression of thought in the final two chapters of that work illustrates this quite clearly.

Religion has to do with the consciousness of absolute being.[7] Thus, wherever there is a form of consciousness of absolute being, however inchoate, there is in some sense religion. The various states of existence of "forms of experience" discussed in the *Phenomenology* — consciousness, self-consciousness, reason and Geist—each express religion differently. At the level of consciousness, religion appears as the consciousness of the supersensuous or "ground of being," the divine as universal, without selfhood (*Bewusstsein des Übersinnlichen, oder Innern des gegenständlichen Daseins.*) With self-consciousness, religion is present as the beyond of the beings towards which the unhappy consciousness strives. Reason strictly speaking has no religious component, because self-consciousness in this form of experience finds itself in "the direct and immediate present." It may perhaps be said to retain religion in that the form of self-consciousness is retained, though "wrongly" directed to the immediate present. Turning to Geist, first in the ethical order, we come across a form of religion, in the belief in fate and the nether world, which becomes a belief in heaven. Because this remains at the level of objectification (understanding) and does not proceed to the unity of subject and object (reason), it disintegrates into the religion of the Enlightenment, in a belief in a heaven or a beyond which is neither needed nor known in any way. From the objective Geist (the ethical order) and Geist as self-alienated, we move to Geist-knowing-itself, which is the level of the pure self-consciousness of Geist: "Geist knowing itself is in religion primarily and immediately its own self-consciousness."[8] The nice distinction made at this point is between Geist and Geist's knowledge or consciousness of self. Thus Hegel can say that the Dasein of Geist is differentiated from its self-consciousness, and hence its actual reality "falls outside religion." In other words, the self-consciousness of Geist is religion, in the sense that it is the consciousness of finite spirits which constitutes the self-consciousness of Geist. The relation to Geist which is this self-consciousness is wholly in history, and is religion: whereas that which it is a relation towards, the being of Geist in itself, stands outside religion, because outside the knowing of finite spirits. It is part of their reality, but not part of their consciousness, at least at the moment of religion. All this can be known because Geist necessarily reveals.[9]

At the same time, the being of Geist and its consciousness of its being are obviously the same, occurring, we might say, in two modes. When the two modes become identical, religion is complete. This is to be achieved by the finite spirits whose consciousness of Geist *is* the self-consciousness of Geist, becoming aware that this is the case. In other words, they come to see that Geist and its self-consciousness, or Geist and its other, are a unity. At that point, absolute knowledge (*absolutes Wissen*) appears, and with it the transition to philosophy, the speculative transformation of the religious standpoint. As we shall see, that crucial step cannot be effected without the role of Christianity, but the moments which precede it in the unfolding of Geist are just as important, since they prepare the way for Christianity. In the *Phenomenology*, these are natural religion, religion in the form of art, and revealed religion. These distinctions are essentially the same as those worked out in fuller detail in the lectures on the philosophy of religion, and we shall comment on them shortly.

The complicated and obscure phraseology of the *Phenomenology* gives way to a clearer, more mature expression in the *Encyclopaedia*:

> Absolute Geist, while it is self-centred identity, is always also identity returning and ever returned into itself: if it is the one and universal *substance* it is so as a spirit, discerning itself into a self and a consciousness, for which it is as substance.[10]

Absolute Geist, as Theunissen points out in his very detailed commentary,[11] is the identity of concept and reality. They are the same; the difference is only that in the reality, the concept is known to be the reality. The unity is perceived in the moment of absolute knowledge. The dialectic of reality, then, does not add anything to Geist beyond the knowledge that it is what it is, beyond a mediated self-consciousness, as opposed to the immediate consciousness of self of subjective Geist. Geist is thereby protected from a material dependence on nature or history. Nevertheless, Geist is also eternal in its returning and in its returned identity; there is thus a sense in which God needs the finite. Without the finite, there would be no mediated consciousness in Geist. God would know self merely immediately. So, Theunissen can say that the primal identity of concept and reality which is absolute Geist, is always already divided into the unity of absolute Geist for self, and absolute Geist's coming to self-consciousness through finite reality.[12]

The first implication, then, of the structure of absolute Geist is that God is both independent of and dependent on the world. The world (objective Geist's field of operations) can have no independence from absolute Geist; to claim that would be to abandon the identity of concept and reality, and so to condemn the world to irrationality. The second consideration that shows up is the question of the relation of the internal structure of divine life and the dialectic, or the connection between immanent and economic. A further implication touches directly on religion, and follows immediately on our previous quotation from Hegel.

> Religion, as this highest plane can in general be referred to, is just as much issuing from the subject and at home there, as to be regarded as issuing objectively from absolute Geist, which is in its community as Geist.[13]

Again, there are two sides to the reality we are considering. If religion is the consciousness *of* Geist, it is so both as subjective and objective genitives: that is, religion is in and issuing from individual finite subjects, in the sense that they are the agents of knowing, of consciousness, which consciousness is the self-consciousness of Geist. And they are and can be this only because Geist is there as a reality in its community, in human history, both in the finite individuals and in the institutions of political and social life.[14] Religion is Geist's *own* consciousness of self. It is, then, not merely an attitude of the individual human being, but an attitude of individuals implanted there by the social reality of Geist into which they are born. Religion is a subjective attitude and objective fact. The individual believer has faith: the community possesses the Geist of truth.[15] This faith grows immediately out of the tension between subjective and objective. It is the individual finite spirit's affirmation of the essential unity of the process, which is of course parallel to such explicitly theological claims as that "God dwells among us," or "God is reconciled with the world," or even "God loves the world."

> Subjective consciousness of absolute Geist is in itself essentially a process, whose immediate and substantial unity is faith in the testimony of Geist as the certainty of the objective truth.[16]

Faith binds the two poles of the individual believer and Geist, both
vertically to Geist as such, and horizontally to the presence of Geist in
the community. The horizontal binding is the cultural form of *Ge-
meinde* or church, the vertical pole is expressed in *Cultus* or worship.
Worship constitutes the attempt of individual and/or community to
overcome the separation between universal and finite. It is a conscious
relation towards the universal:

> Faith, at once this immediate unity, and containing it as the relation
> to each varied determination, is transformed in worship, explicit or
> implicit *cultus*, into the process of raising the antithesis to the level of
> spiritual liberation, of validating the initial certainty through this
> mediation, and of attaining to the concrete determination
> itself—reconciliation, the actuality of Geist.[17]

Hegel's picture of the reality of religion, then, is of a community of
individuals, bound together by their individual faith in the relation
of the divine to them, and in their confidence that the divine is present in that community. The community expresses its desire to be
united with or reconciled to that divine which is both distinct from it,
and yet one with it, in its worship. Moreover, the faith and worship
join to overcome the finite representationalism which presents God to
consciousness as a "mental representation" (*Vorstellung*).[18]

In the *Encyclopaedia*, as a formal philosophical work, Hegel moves
away from the introductory material we have just considered to trace
the knowledge of the absolute in the field of art, where it is divided
into its constituent parts in the finitude of the work of art, yet points
towards the infinite in the contemplation of the idea that a work of
art offers. This orientation towards the universal leads art to pass
naturally into religion, and in the third part of the *Encyclopaedia*
Hegel deals only with *revealed* religion, "the religion whose content is
absolute Geist."[19] Religion itself gives way to philosophy as the cognition "of the necessity in the content of the picture-idea" or
Vorstellung.[20] Just as the lectures on the philosophy of history take up
the material of objective Geist and represent the logical dialectic in a
chronological sequence, so the lectures on the philosophy of religion
constitute the same process for the material of absolute Geist. The
text of the lectures is complex and unsatisfactorily presented in

English,[21] and by no means perfect in German, but it seems probable that Hegel presented introductory material on the concept of religion, and then discussed the history of religion, taking in turn natural religion (primitive religions), determinate religion (Greek, Roman, Jewish), and the absolute or perfected religion (Christianity). The purpose and progress of the work is also identical to the lectures on the philosophy of history; that is, the data of history furnish the evidence in their own way for the truth presented conceptually in the *Encyclopaedia*, the results of which are expressed without the "proof" in the introductory material to the lectures on the philosophy of religion.

These lectures lay out more clearly and at greater length the conception of religion. As concept, it has the three moments of universality, particularity or differentiation, and the return to the universal in the overcoming (*Aufhebung*) of the differentiation. The first or universal moment is that of thought thinking itself, "the moment of thought in its complete universality."[22] The object, the universal, thought, is the same as the subject, the universal, the thought thinking. It is not a thought *of* anything, since that would be to introduce the idea of differentiation and to move on to the second moment. In other words, the first moment is that of God as self-thinking thought or unmediated self-consciousness. Moreover, if this is the universal, then the religion of the human subject in its vertical dimension will be a "rising up to the true," and not a reference to another sensuous or finite object. The relation of finite subject to infinite object will then be a relation of a moment in the process to the whole process, not a relation of one discrete object to another. As a corollary to this, too, the element of thought becomes *the* medium of religion, rather than something alien to it:

> God is not the highest feeling, but the highest thought; if God is indeed also lowered to the level of a representation, the content of this representation certainly belongs to the level of thought. The silliest mistake of our times is the opinion that thought is detrimental to religion, and that the more thought is abandoned, the more secure religion is.[23]

The universal is the unmediated identity of subject and object, of thought as thinker and thought as that which is thought. And the process by which it comes to a mediated identity will be the acting out or externalization of that internal relationship. The second moment is thus the moment of differentiation, the recognition of that which is thought as different from the thinker of the thought. This particularization is the appearance of the finite level of the other. Here we deal with consciousness in individuality rather than universality, and with the immediate finite subject, as conscious of the difference between infinite and finite. This is treated in a justly famous and genuinely poetic passage, in terms of the individual finite subject's being the two sides of the relation, two sides which seek each other and flee from each other, the finite and the infinite in the human. The human ego is the relations, the perception of their unity and their conflict, and the recognition that both are fully real, that "I" am "I" in either:

> I am not one of those comprised within the struggle, but I am both combatants, and the combat itself. I am the fire and the water which touch one another, and the touching and unity of those things which simply flee from one another, and even this touching is itself this double, essentially antagonistic relation, as the relation of what is now separated, severed, now reconciled and united with itself.[24]

The finite subject over against the absolute knows itself as a moment, and therefore as not necessary or eternal, but as having its true being in the absolute substance. The recognition of this initiates the activity of restoration and possession, and this is worship. Worship does not then simply mean the outward acts, but also the internal progress, insofar as these represent the movement towards the restoration of the unity. Clearly, then, the sacramental and other worship of the church is paralleled by the development of an "inward history," conversion of spirit, or thought, as far as it contributes to that history. These two go together; it is wrong to see religion as purely subjective or purely objective. On the one hand, human consciousness cannot attain to objective knowledge of an absolute object; on the other, subjective knowledge attains to nothing outside the conscousness at all. Clearly, worship and idea or representation are related:

> What a human being believes he or she has to do in relation to God, corresonds with the representation of God. . . . Only when religion is a true

relation and incorporates the difference at the level of consciousness, can worship be the *Aufhebung* of the severed into a living process.[25]

Worship is defined as "the eternal process of the subject, to make itself identical with its essential being."[26] It is the bringing together of the severed parts, finite human subject and absolute object, in the finite human subject who is also a moment in the absolute. But it does not, as it may seem, belong only to the subjective side of the dualism—for the unity to be attained in the subject's worship, it must have existed originally in and for itself.[27] This can be clarified by looking at the opposite possibility: if there had never been a unity in the infinite of finite and infinite, then the finite could not itself effect such a relation. It would always be a relation to a mere object, which is in fact the relation of finite to bad (i.e., non-inclusive) infinite.[28] But it is quite within the compass of a finite that is a moment in the infinite, to come to a consciousness of a relation which has a prior existence in the object itself. Hegel gives the obvious example, which we shall come to shortly, of the Christian understanding of incarnation.

What is Christianity for Hegel?

The course of history, as we noted above, demonstrates the theoretical construction of religious reality. Determinate religions constitute successive attempts of Geist to establish the identity of concept and reality, to move the actual religions of the world to represent the truth of the conception of religion (outlined above). The various conceptions which precede Christianity are in some way incomplete: thus, the Jewish God is the unity, but an abstract unity, because it does not exist as a concrete unity, i.e., there is no incarnation. The Greek religion, on the other hand, managed to achieve an idea of the divine as subject, but only as one subject among many, one god among many. And the problem with the Roman religion is that it subordinates the divine to an external purpose, i.e, the building of empire. The crucial point about Christianity, however, is that it is a *revealed* religion.

Hegel is not concerned with revelation as, for example, propositional, or contained in the Bible, but with the idea that it is because it is the nature of God to reveal, that the conception of the true religion must be that of a revealed religion. Knowledge is what makes the eternal substance Geist, and the essence of knowledge is self-realization. It starts out as knowledge knowing itself and achieves its mediated knowledge, necessary for its full actuality, through the moment of externalization or manifestation:

> Geist is only Geist inasmuch as it is for Geist; and in the absolute religion it is absolute Geist, which no longer manifests its abstract moments, but rather itself.[29]

One of the major implications of this understanding of God is that the divine is knowable. "Natural theology" is not only a possibility, but is in most respects identical with speculative philosophy. It can be so precisely because God's essence is self-revelation, and therefore human knowing, the "common medium" of the human and the divine, so to speak, constitutes knowledge of and access to divine reality, or Geist. Hegel considers that the theologian who claims human being knows nothing of God is shirking the task of theology. The finite representationalism with which human beings work in religion, we have already seen, tends towards being overcome in worship, and also in thought, the internal correlate of public worship. For Hegel, devotion and theology are not alien to one another.

Once again, however, this human knowing of God is the divine self-knowledge in its finite moment. The revelation of what Geist is, in the world, is as much for Geist itself as it is for finite spirits. Geist would be what it is without such a revelation, and would even know itself unmediatedly, unconsciously. But without revelation, or without religion, it would not be for itself, would not know its essential being consciously:

> This knowledge of Geist for itself of what it is in itself, is the potential and actual being of knowing Geist, the perfect, absolute religion, in which it is manifest what Geist, God, is; this is the Christian religion.[30]

Of course, this can be so for Hegel because the characteristics of Christianity as he understands it meet exactly the abstract concept of religion and thus constitute its actualization:

God is this: distinguishing from self, making self an object, but in this distinction purely identical with self—Geist.[31]

Christianity is the absolute religion for no other reason than that the "economy of salvation" in Christianity corresponds to this abstract concept. Hegel represents the three moments variously: as thought, representation and feeling; as God in eternity "before" the creation of the world, God as creator, and God as reconciler; as the Father, the Son and the Spirit. As Hodgson points out in his appendix to his edition of part three of the lectures on religion,[32] this constitutes a specific trinitarian designation for the first time, and raises in classical trinitarian terms the question of the relation of God and world.

The major point to remember is that God is defined as self-knowledge, self-consciousness, and so in othering self, God is establishing an externalized structure parallel to the internal "organization" of the divine. In more Hegelian terms, the logical Idea alienates or objectifies itself. And to put it slightly differently again, it is the nature of God to be self-expression or revelation, and therefore what is expressed or revealed is God. The abstract or internal or subjective is made concrete, external, objective. In the consequent recognition that the two sides are one, the reconciliation which establishes the concrete, mediated self-consciousness is achieved. The moment of differentiation of the divine involves a bifurcation, because there are two ways or modes in which God can posit an other. God can first of all be opposed as that which is the other of God as Geist—which is nature. Or God can be opposed as the other of God as infinite—this is finite spirit. And the true other of God is thus the unity of the two, or world. As the opposite of Geist the world is not a part of God, but separate, the realm of nature (thus saving the accusation of pantheism), and as the opposite of infinite it is yet a *finite* Geist (thus saving mere objectivity, which would render reconciliation impossible). Moreover, this othering of God is a *self*-othering, and so that which is alien is also a moment in God.

As we have already seen, religion involves the consciousness on the part of finite spirit of the relation of unity between Geist in itself, God, and the world of finite individuals. If we ask the transcendental question, what would make possible such a consciousness, then the answer is clearly, such a revelation of God's essential being as would be accessible to the finite individual. Such a revelation would have to be itself finite, or it could not be received by a finite individual, i.e., it would have to occur in history. And yet it would have to be a revelation of the self of God, or a further revelation would be necessary to reveal the truth of this revelation. Therefore, if the finite human consciousness is to become conscious of the true relation between Geist as such and the finite spirits, which is a necessary moment in the self-realization of Geist, its becoming absolute Geist, then there must be in history a true revelation of the being of God. This is essentially what the Incarnation means to Hegel.

Hegel takes it that all religions have some sense of incarnation wherever there is talk of unity between God and human being. This has to do with the "other side" of the Incarnation, the significance of the Incarnation for God, which occurs in the context of Geist coming to contemplate itself, for which it must posit itself as other. The perfect other of God is God in the other, or Geist present in the world in full estrangement from self. Geist cannot be not-Geist, and therefore cannot be its perfect other as nature—we have already seen that that would be pantheism. So Geist is its other as Geist within nature, as non-infinite. Geist is totally objective to itself as finite spirit for whom Geist itself, God, is known as other, and for which finite consciousness, its own finitude, is a contingent moment in Geist. God, so to speak, in finite subjectivity, is at first merely for-self, quite unconscious of the in-and-for-selfness which is to come about through this moment. In the words of scripture, "God empties himself, taking the form of a slave, being born in the likeness of sinful man . . ." Something must happen for the finite subject to become aware of the identity, and this seems to mean that something must happen to the consciousness of Jesus if he is to become aware of his messianic role, still more so if he is to be said to be aware in any sense at all of his "divinity." If this were not so, then the unity of consciousness between Jesus and God would disrupt God's perfect othering. Hegel did not see this problem, and, as we shall see in a moment, gave a great deal of emphasis to the Johannine Jesus in consequence.

Hegel's concern in chapter four of the final part of the lectures on religion (on Hodgson's numbering)[33] is to demonstrate the pattern by which reconciliation is achieved. With James Yerkes, we can say that the religious character of human being as rational manifests itself initially in the "consciousness that the immediately apparent is not the metaphysically ultimate." Hegel frequently makes use of the idea that to conceive of a limit as a limit it is necessary to be beyond it. Thus the human being can move from immediate, sensuous, individual things to God as the ground of the finite. This, which from the side of the finite is the ability to conceive of the infinite, is from the side of the absolute, a capacity for the divine in the finite.[34] A "capacity for the divine" is another way to say "implicit unity." Obviously this anthropological pattern is not peculiar to Christian men and women alone, and hence the idea of divine-human implicit unity and even incarnation, as we have already seen, is not restricted to Christianity. However, the revelation that this implicit unity does truly exist must come to human beings from outside their own minds. The human mind can think the possibility, formulate the hypothesis, or it could not recognize it when it happened, but it cannot provide the actuality. Hence, the unity of human and divine has to be disclosed in "a wholly temporal, completely common worldly appearance in one particular man."[35] Hegel represents this more theoretically as the principle that the human being can only posit reconciliation for himself or herself on the presupposition that "precisely what is posited is also something implicit":

> The truth must therefore appear to the subject as a presupposition, and the question is how and in what form the truth might appear in connection with the standpoint we now occupy.[36]

And, of course, the form of appearance of the truth must be that of certainty, not that of speculative thinking or philosophy. It achieves certainty only in "immediate, sensible perception and external existence":

> Only what exists in an immediate way, in inner or outer perception, is certain. In order for this divine-human unity to become certain for humanity, God had to appear in the world in the flesh. . . . At the same time it should be added that the unity of divine and human nature must appear in a single man.[37]

The individuality of the appearance is intrinsically connected with its concreteness. Only as one individual is the abstractness of the universal escaped. And, finally, if we ask why God had to appear as a human being, well, God had to be sensibly present for reconciliation to occur, and since in the sensible order human being alone is spiritual (*geistig*), God had to become human being.

> God appears in sensible presence; God has no other form than that of the sensible mode of Geist, which is that of an individual human being—this is the only sensible form of Geist.[38]

How is the individual made aware that Jesus is the divine Idea? Hegel suggests two ways, the content of his teaching and the form of his life. The teaching has a limited value, since it "affects only the imagination" when taken alone, and does not have the dimension of story or history. It is just as well that Hegel gives a lesser place to the teaching, since much of what he assigns to Jesus, later generations of scripture scholars would question. Nevertheless, there is an uncanny modernity in the aspects which Hegel singles out for comment. He selects three: the moral imperative expressed as love of neighbour; a revolutionary attitude towards established orders, as a result of the primacy of love; and the authentic characteristic of the kingdom of God, that is, "the relationship of Christ himself to God and of humanity to God and Christ."[39]

The major problem with Hegel's treatment of the teaching of Jesus is his dependence on the God-man of Johannine tradition. For Hegel, Jesus is aware of his relation to the Father, and of his own "majesty of spirit."[40] But it is not clear to me that this is a substantive problem in Hegel's thought. Jesus Christ is after all not the concept, not present in the form of thinking, but a sensible immediacy, God as a human being, and therefore subject not only to suffering and death, but to the inevitable limitations of historicity. In other words, I see no reason why Hegel's Jesus could not be what he was without being speculatively aware of what he was. Surely if he was fully aware, and yet he was a human being, as Hegel insists, he would have anticipated the arrival of Hegelian speculative philosophy. A truer understanding of the Johannine emphases, which would still leave room for a Hegelian interpretation, is to see them as reflections on the status of Jesus as representation (*Vorstellung*) of God—thus John pursues his own speculative transformation of the figure of Jesus into a divine Logos.[41] Our fusion of horizons with Hegel licenses us to read the philosopher through an appreciation of historicity to which he could not have been party.

The more significant aspect of Jesus' existence for Hegel is the form or history, especially of his death. In the first place, it is "the seal of his teaching . . . an example . . . of the love that marked his conduct."[42] However, the crucial point has to do with the speculative significance of Christ. It will be remembered that the Incarnation is the othering of Geist, the objectivation of subjective Geist in its other, finitude. Hence, a total sharing in finitude involves a sharing in death, "the highest pinnacle of finitude."[43] In this ultimate moment of negation is revealed the "highest divestment of the divine Idea," the death of God. It is complete estrangement, but at the same time the highest love, "for love consists in giving up one's personality, all that is one's own, etc."[44] Moreover, the absolute history of the divine Idea can only be presented in a single human being because of the human potential for union with the divine, or, to put it in more Hegelian terms, with the intrinsic human relation to the concept:

> Thus, my eating an apple means that I destroy its organic self-identity and assimilate it to myself. That I can do this entails that the apple in itself . . . has in its nature the determination of being something that has in itself a homogeneity with the digestive process such that I can make it homogeneous with myself.[45]

With the crucifixion, God is dead, but God so to speak "maintains self in this process,"[46] and the resurrection is revealed as the death of death. But with the resurrection, the appearance of God in the flesh, which has occurred under the conditions of humanity, comes to an end and, like all sensible presence, "It passes by as something for itself and becomes past history."[47] And with the passing of sensible presence, the move from externality to internality, comes the point of the formation of the community under the guidance of the Spirit. In other words, with the end of Jesus Christ's sensible presence in human history, with the death and all it means, the community of faith is born, living by the spirit of Christ. This community is in its turn the community which lives by the presence of the Spirit, and by worship as a sacramental partaking of/or communion in the mystical union of divine and human.[48]

So far, then, we have seen how Hegel establishes a view of the abstract conception of religion as the attitude of finite spirits towards Geist, within the process by which Geist comes to mediated self-consciousness. Indeed, religion *is* the process, looked at from the side of the finite spirits who constitute the moment of consciousness in the passage from unmediated to mediated or absolute Geist. And we have gone on to see Hegel's view of Christianity as the absolute religion, i.e., that Christianity is the actualization of this abstract conception of religion in its perfection. Of course, Christianity remains a religion; it exists at the level of a representational presentation of the truth. But as a perfect representation of the idea, it places before the human subject the material for the speculative transformation of religion into its truth, the concept. It is, in other words, the material on which philosophy can work.

We shall go a little further into the relations of religion and philosophy in the fourth part of this chapter. For the moment we turn instead to the question of religion and the state. To introduce this, we need simply to reflect back on the discussion of Hegel's views of religion. The abstract concept of religion is expressed and understood in terms of the overall dialectic. Religion does not occupy a private realm, nor is it a special way of looking at reality. It is the true recognition and response of finite spirit to the infinite. It is the human consciousness of overall spiritual reality. It is, it seems, an anthropological structure before it is an institution, although as will be remembered from chapter one, human beings only achieve true humanity in a true community, and so we can expect a relationship to be revealed between the anthropological structures of Hegelian human being, and the shape of the community. Just such a relationship exists between the state as the ethical substance, and the individual finite wills which comprise its actuality.

Religion and the State

There are four major discussions in Hegel's mature writings of the relationship between religion and the state.[49] I shall begin with that in the *Encyclopaedia*, and then fill it out from the *Philosophy of Right*, finally glancing at the lectures on the philosophy of religion and of history to see what they may add. In the third part of the *Encyclopaedia*, the subject is treated in the context of considering the ethical life. The starting-point is finite, the "real ethical self-consciousness," which rises to its truth, like everything else in the system, by passing through its negative pole. The negative pole of ethical self-consciousness is the state of freedom from subjectivity and selfish desire. We have already encountered it as the individual's participation in the ethical life of the state, the perfection of the consonance between the individual and the universal, the true freedom of finite spirits. This conscious relation back to the universal is the same move that we have just seen made in Hegel's explication of religion from the side of finite spirit. The ethical life and religion are ways of referring to the same essential process—the raising of finite Geist to its truth:

> True religion and true religiosity come only from the ethical life, and are the thinking ethical life, the free universality becoming conscious of its concrete essence. Only from and through the ethical life is the idea of God known to be free Geist; outside the ethical Geist it is fruitless to go looking for true religion and religiosity.[50]

In being ethical, the individual ethical subject has passed through the negation of self to the point of crossing over to the essence of the ethical life itself. Thus, it is through the ethical life that the individual comes to true religion.

This is not to say that religion depends on ethics, but that access to the truth of religion is through the ethical life and its implications. In fact, there is a reciprocal relationship, since although true religion is reached through reflection on the ethical life, when reached it is revealed to be the ground of ethical values, since it is the consciousness of absolute truth. In other words, the ethical life is the logically dependent, although true religion is the chronologically subsequent. Ethical values are thus true insofar as they participate in the consciousness of absolute truth, and the content of religion must be true and real (that is, its idea of God must be the true idea) if the truly moral life is to be lived. Religion is "the thinking ethical life," and the ethical life is "the divine Geist as indwelling the self-consciousness." Reflection upon the ethical life reveals the indwelling of the divine Geist, and issues in a religious relation to Geist. The two are inseparable, and for self-consciousness religion is "the basis of the ethical life and of the state."[51]

This mutuality is the key to Hegel's understanding of the relations of religion and the state. Religion can become a bondage to a body of truth which is presented as external to self-consciousness. If truth is represented as something over against the individual, God is presented as an external thing (Hegel's example here would be the Catholic doctrine of the eucharist); truth is passed to the rank of the laity from the rank of the clergy; there grows up a legislative and constitutional system which builds this bondage of the spirit into the political life of the nation, and leads to ethical principles which are negative to true self-consciousness. They encourage holiness rather than the ethical life—chastity and not marriage, a vow of poverty instead of industry and honesty in daily life, and a vow of obedience to external authority rather than an internal obedience to that law and legal arrangement of the state which is in fact true freedom, since it expresses in institutional form the truth of human nature.

If, however, the divine Geist is allowed to interpenetrate the entirety of secular life, then the virtues of the individual self-consciousness, those which are natural to it, are the virtues of religion—marriage, the ethical life in the social world, and obedience to (natural) law. Because the true ethical life is grounded only in the true religion, therefore both religion and *Sittlichkeit* must promote the spirit's essential liberty:

> It is a foolish idea to want to allocate separate areas for the state and religion, in the opinion that their differences can exist quietly side by side, and not break out in conflict and war.[52]

Nevertheless, religion has its distinct limitations, and this becomes much clearer in the treatment of the same relation in the *Philosophy of Right*, to which we now turn. The major limitation is that it is

> a relation to the Absolute, a relation which takes the form of feeling, representative thinking, faith; and, brought within its all-embracing circumference, everything becomes only accidental and transient.[53]

Thus, if we insist on looking at the state from this viewpoint, the state comes to seem accidental and transient, weak. The form of religion "comes to be purely subjective" but the laws in the state are objective and universal. So the state, *der Geist der in der Welt steht,*[54] stands as the objective presentation of what is presented subjectively in religion:

> The genuine truth is the prodigious transfer of the inner into the outer, the building of reason into the real world, and this has been the task of the world during the whole course of its history.[55]

This is a most important point for our purposes in the entire work in hand, and needs to be stressed. The state is the presentation in objective, institutional structures, of the truth available subjectively in the religious impulse. It might be a temptation to take the church to be that institutionalization of the truth, but this is not the case. The church is the community of those who respond religiously to the truth, both individually and as a community in worship. The church, in other words, structures the religious response. But the truth of religion becomes available in the world only when Geist is allowed to interpenetrate the entirety of secular life, and this occurs whenever and wherever the idea of the state is brought to actuality. Of course, the actualization of the idea of the state, like the reality of the religious response, is the work of individual finite subjects. It can therefore be claimed that personal and corporate religion, like personal ethical judgment and the corporate building of the true idea of human nature as community in the state, are two modes of human involvement in the divine reality. We shall return to this subject—secularization—in the next chapter.

The lengthy excursus which now follows in the *Philosophy of Right* concentrates much more on the interrelations of church and state within community, than it refers to the essential reciprocity of religion and the state. When the religious impulse is organized in the form of an institution, as a church, it naturally comes in large measure under the control of the state. It has to obey the laws of property, for example, if it possesses any, and it has to bow to the state when the doctrine it teaches out of subjective conviction touch on objective principles, "thoughts of the ethical and rational." The church retains the faith and authority "in matters affecting ethical principles" and laws, but under the form of subjective conviction, whereas "the state is that which knows."[56] There is no doubt that the state has the last word:

> the state retains the right and the form of self-conscious, objective rationality, the right to make this form count and to maintain it against pretentions springing from truth in a subjective dress, no matter how such truth may gird itself with certitude and authority.[57]

We need to remain very clear about the distinction between religion and the church; the church is one particular community, existing in a specific time and place within one particular state. Nowhere, as far as I can discover, does Hegel suggest that the perfect church exists or has existed. Certainly, the absolute religion has come to be, with the speculative truth about reality present in representative form in Christianity, and therefore the *idea* is perfected. But the actualization in history can only ever be a finite, and therefore imperfect, actualization.

The material presented in the lectures on religion is essentially a reworking of what we have so far seen in the *Encyclopaedia* and the *Philosophy of Right*.[58] This time the common essence of state and religion is expressed as their relation to freedom. In religion, the individual finite subject comes to know God as free Geist, and to bring self into conformity with the divine will, or to appreciate their implicit unity. In doing this, the finite subject annuls the division between absolute will and self, and shares the freedom of Geist. The state is freedom, but in the moment of actuality. It is the truth of the divine free Geist, translated into the institutions of human society—free structures. Within human history, then, the relation of finite subject to free Geist in religion is paralleled by the relation of the same subject to the objective institutionalization of the free Geist. This is what it means for the state to be "Geist on earth." The true state institutionalizes divine freedom, so that in concrete existence the finite subject can also be free.

In the lectures on the philosophy of history, Hegel argues that that which comes to be an object of consciousness in the state is the total culture (*Bildung*) of the nation. The express consciousness of the *Volksgeist*, which is the substance of *Bildung*, is achieved through religion: "Religion is the place where a people gives itself the definition of what it holds to be true."[59] If this is so, then religion is close to politics, because it is the basis of freedom: if freedom is genuine, it must have its grounding in the true. Its absolute validity can only come from its universal principle. So the state as the realm of freedom rests on religion, the principle of freedom.

We are now approaching the point in this work where explication of Hegel will begin to give way to a more constructive attempt to situate some of what we have seen in a wider and more explicitly theological context. It therefore seems an appropriate stage at which to draw together in summary form what has already been proposed.

We began essentially by focusing on the concept of the state through a series of eccentric circles, each one of which was included inside the surface area of its precedent. The circular process of the entire dialectic led us to a consideration of the parallel internal dialectic of Geist, then to the realm of objective Geist as constituted by the dialectical progression of absolute right, morality and *Sittlichkeit*. And finally we discovered the state as the third term in the ethical life, the unity of family and civil society. If we were to lay out the successive stages of Hegel's *Encyclopaedia* in a list, then the state would be simply swallowed up in the details which surround it. But as our analysis in chapter two progressed, it became apparent how crucial the state is for human meaning, for a life lived in accordance with human being's true nature. The current emphasis in philosophy and theology on "human being in community," or sociality, is only a modern form of Hegel's insistence that true human essence and freedom is made possible only in the state.

Of course, this realization of what the state is, is not a realization for which the state is itself responsible. It is part of the reflection on human subjectivity and divine subjectivity that only occurs at the moment of speculative philosophy, and this in its turn is a product of the human subject as a religious being, rising to thinking about the representation of truth in the absolute religion, Christianity. Having reached the concept, the speculative transformation of religion, the human subject can then in principle uncover the rationality or the spiritual quality of human institutions, and so, for example, is in a position to see how the idea of the state conforms to the absolute idea, and, indeed, how and why religion is the ground of the state.

At this point we need to ask again about the nature and the relations of religion and the state, but this time from the point of view of the finite subject. *Vis-a-vis* religion (and now we are concerned only with Christianity, the absolute religion), the finite subject comes to a conviction of the implicit unity of human and divine. He or she recognizes the validation of truth and freedom in a revealed relation to absolute truth and freedom. This relation constitutes human beings in a community which is marked by the recognition of the relationship, or the recognition of the presence of Geist within it. In worship the subjective affirmation of the relationship is expressed collectively. From religion, then, human beings acquire a feeling of potential unity with the divine, and this is the faith conviction. But the subjective relationship, although of course it makes life intelligible, does not give shape to ordinary day-to-day living. If everyday life is to acquire the form of rationality, the newly-revealed relationship of freedom and incorporation must take the form of *law*, adherence to which will cement the implicit union of human and divine expressed most directly in religion. It is the role of the state, as ethical substance, to express this union concretely. Consequently, we can now tentatively propose that human sociality in a true community is the actualization of the religious relationship.

All this is only true for Hegel in dealing with true religion. Religion is a relationship to Geist, and human life in general is affected by that relationship, the central anthropological motif. Hegel does not and cannot express human nature except in terms of Geist and of sociality, exactly the terms in which he discusses religion. The admission of God or Geist to all aspects of human existence is a precondition for their meaning anything at all. And their objectivation of divine truth gives them a certain superiority over the subjectivity of "purely" religious motivation. Religion in the sense in which the word might be most immediately understood today, the activity of and emotions associated with going to church, is but one form of what Hegel calls religion. Religion is life seen as a search for and a living out of the true relationship of human being to the absolute, and the discovery that in the structures of human being lies the condition of possibility of seeing the value of the search at all. Religion lies in the anthropological structures of human being much more crucially and genuinely than in the churches. Of course, the realization that this is the case is the insight of the few who have gone beyond religion to its speculative transformation. But this going beyond, although it means the end of religion as the ultimate expression of truth, yet only makes explicit or clarifies the truth of religion, and in no way contradicts it.

Will Religion Last?
Its Relation to Philosophy

A lot of ink has been spilled over the relation of religion and philosophy in Hegel's system.[60] There are two possible understandings of Hegel's position—philosophy can be seen as having replaced religion, at least in principle, or it can be seen as having presented the truth of religion in a different and fuller form, but without displacing it. Of course, Hegel did not claim that religion had disappeared, but it could be argued that he claimed it had reached the end of its usefulness, because speculative thought is the distillation in the form of the concept of the truth held by religion in the form of representation. Religion has the truth, but only philosophy knows the truth. Hegel's notorious "discordant note"[61] is also concerned with the move from religion to philosophy, but it should not be forgotten that he is discussing a corrupt form of religion, one in which the clergy or leaders have wandered off along their own speculative lines, and abandoned the mass of people who cannot achieve a "concrete, everinsistent reason." What should happen is that "instead of allowing reason and religion to contradict themselves," we ought to seek "reconciliation in the form of philosophy."[62]

Hegel does not spell out how he proposes to do that. Solving the problems of the present day is not the role of philosophy. In fact, "in philosophy itself the resolution is only partial."[63] The point, I take it, is that philosophy itself is a speculative transformation of religious truth, and so would be self-contradictory if it then turned back to the form of religion which it had left behind. On the other hand, speculative philosophy, in demonstrating the implicit rationality of religion, offers itself as a potential reconciler of the apparent gulf between religion and reason. It is certainly not the role of philosophers themselves to do this, for they are "an isolated order of priests."[64] And it is certainly not possible for the majority of the people to see the truth in any other way than in the form of representation. The possibility of the community perishing is mentioned but not pursued, and Hegel certainly did not think that religion as a cultural form would ever disappear. But what precisely he intended at this point is not very clear.

Whatever it was, it is quite certain that his world is one in which religion and speculative philosophy *de facto* co-exist, and in which the initiative has passed to the latter, although it performs in its way what religion did or does in its. The question can therefore legitimately be asked, just what role and reality religion retains in the "new" world of speculative thought. When Hegel says that "religion must take refuge in philosophy," and that "from the point of view of the world, a passing away takes place in it, but this concerns only its form of externality, of contingent occurrence,"[65] he is clearly not arguing for a total disappearance. He is, rather, suggesting that the essential religious impulse persists in the new age in which philosophy reconciles religion and reason, in which philosophy as a reflective activity has interpreted "the truth of what-is" in perfect conformity with the representations of the religious imagination and *Cultus*. But is this become a religion of the mind alone? Possibly for the speculative philosopher, but not for the masses. And the religious community which continues in the old ways cannot be a mere redundant pageant, because although it represents the truth in an incomplete form, it continues to represent the truth, and to be the subjective and emotional underpinning to the ethical life. That role never passes away.

This fact is rarely recognized in discussions of religion and philosophy in the Hegelian vision. If we look at the end of the lectures on religion or at the *Encyclopaedia*, we may get the impression that with the appearance of speculative philosophy, religion melts into insignificance. But we have seen the place of religion discussed as a factor in the life of the state, and in the coming to consciousness of individual finite spirits. And such a discussion of the place of religion as a permanent feature in existence is only possible from the standpoint of speculative philosophy. Hegel's consistent method is to discuss a logical sequence as if it were a chronological development. What has to be proved is always presupposed at the beginning, and used throughout. The primacy of the self-thinking thought, of absolute knowledge, is operative throughout the discussion even of the early stages of the system, because it is as an approach to the possession of absolute knowledge that the system exists. Therefore it is contradictory to talk of religion as if it were destined to disappear at the logical culmination of the system, when the absolute knowledge that emerges at this culmination has already constructed a chronological picture in which religion has a permanent place and a role in and opposite to the state.

On the other hand, Hegel does say that there is a passing away in at least the form of religion, and that it must "take refuge in philosophy." This recalls our earlier distinction between religion and church, or between the idea of religion and the cultural form that it has taken in Christendom. The point of religion is that it is the place where the finite subject comes to see his or her incorporation implicitly in absolute truth, and expresses that reference to truth in worship, and thence in thought. There is an obvious sense in which the conceptual grasp of the latter in philosophy supersedes the representative imaging of it in religion. Yet the reference back in worship cannot be superseded as a social phenomenon. Worship is the community achieving together what the individual may achieve in thought. And worship is one dimension singularly lacking in the realm of speculative philosophy, perhaps precisely because community itself is absent. In philosophy there is only an isolated order of priests, a gnostic minority who know what the majority cannot know. Yet although the majority cannot know this, since this truth is dispersed in different ways in the normal social forms of ethical life and religion, the majority can share fully in that truth.

It seems that religion is a permanent feature in the social structure of Hegel's world. That picture of society is laid out not in the passages dealing with absolute Geist, or in the lectures on the philosophy of religion, but in the treatment of objective Geist. The sections of the *Encyclopaedia*, for example, which succeed the discussion of objective Geist, constitute only the explanation for the absolute validity of what is there contained. From the standpoint of the finite subject, his or her incorporation as a moment in the self-consciousness of absolute Geist does not remove the reality of his or her particular situation, but on the contrary validates it as of absolute, if finite, significance. Religion could be said to be the socialization of this insight, and certainly the insight, although a reference to a beyond, has its importance for the validation of the here and now.

By such a roundabout path we have finally come to a point at which we can mention the term "secularization." We shall have to consider in the following pages several understandings of the term, but we can safely say in advance that it has to do with the validation of the here and now, whether it ends by giving a negative or positive value to religion in that process. Before we turn to these secularization theories themselves, I should like to prepare the way by examining the sociological perspective of Thomas Luckmann,[66] which sheds considerable light on the continuing role of religion and in particular on the placing of the essentially religious at a far more primordial level than that of the ecclesial community itself.

Luckmann sets out to consider contemporary socialization, believing with Durkheim and Weber that religion is the key to the understanding of the social location of the individual.[67] His initial attack is on the superficiality of sociological theory in its equation of secularization with decline in church attendance, and the consequent assumption that modern society is non-religious.[68] This, he believes, has two damaging consequences: firstly, the techniques of institutional analysis are taken to be adequate to the entire study of religion; and secondly, this means that *de facto* the sociologists accept the self-interpretation and ideology of religious institutions. They are begging one important question, according to Luckmann: "What are the conditions under which 'transcendent,' superordinated and 'integrating' structures of meaning are socially objectivated?"[69] By missing this question, sociological theory has been in error:

> . . . It has prejudged the answer to the question whether, in contemporary society, any socially objectivated meaning structures but the

traditional institutionalized religious doctrines function to integrate the routines of everyday life and to legitimate its crises.[70]

And so it fails to deal with the all-important question, with the "essentially . . . religious aspects of the location of the individual in society." It could be argued, rightly I think, that Luckmann is himself at this point guilty of begging questions; in particular, whether religion is *about* transcendent, superordinated and integrating structures of meaning. Since this is essentially in line with the Hegelian view of religion, Luckmann's deficiency in this regard need not detain us.

Luckmann is, of course, quite correct in seeing that the decline in church attendance is significant. It shows, for example, that "the configuration of meaning which constitutes the symbolic reality of traditional church religion appears to be unrelated to the culture of modern industrial society."[71] In his opinion, this alone is sufficient to explain the marginal status of traditional church religion in contemporary society, without having to invoke anti-religious ideologies. This marginality raises two questions: the causes of the phenomenon must be uncovered, and secondly, "it is necessary to ask whether anything that could be called religion in the framework of sociological analysis replaced traditional church religion in modern society."[72]

Already, we can see the parallel with Hegel. Luckmann's intent is to use sociological analysis to uncover a more primary religious reality than that represented by church as institution. His implied definition of religion turns him immediately to human integration in the social world, and to the anthropological structures which underpin such a conception. He rightly sees that both questions touch on the problem of secularization. The point of view of the churches, which Luckmann argues is swallowed whole by the generality of sociologists of religion, is that decline in religion is measurable by dwindling congregations, and that this equals secularization. But on the hypothesis suggested by Luckmann, secularization would be equivalent to uncovering a deeper meaning of religion than merely institutional religion. Secularization would on this theory, if proved correct, be a positive step towards rescuing religion from cultural decline, or what Hegel called "perishing." I would like simply to suggest at this point that for religion to take shelter under the umbrella of philosophy, which is

Hegel's solution for its sickness, is one form of implementing Luckmann's proposal. Whether they go further together we shall now see.

Luckmann determines to seek back behind the ethnocentricity of the substantive definition of religion arrived at under the all-pervasive influence of Christianity, to find a functional definition of more generality. This involves considering as problematic the general anthropological conditions for whatever it is that finally becomes institutionalized in religion, and its reality prior to that institutionalization. Behind these questions he finds the even more general question of "how symbolic universes in general, and a religious cosmos in particular, are socially objectivated."[73] These symbolic universes are "objectivated meaning-systems that relate the experiences of everyday life to a 'transcendent' layer of reality." The component objectivations are:

> products of subjective activities that become available as elements in a common world both to their producers and to other men. While expressions are available only in face-to-face situations, objectivations serve as indices of meaning outside such limitations of space and time. Objectivations are essentially social.[74]

According to Luckmann, these objectivations occur in the transcending of purely biological nature by the human organism. Biologically, we could learn from past experiences, but not build frameworks of interpretation: "a human organism considered in a rigorously biological perspective would be wrapped up, as it were, in the immediacy of ongoing experiences."[75] But all the peculiarly human abilities—abstraction, learning from the past, positing the future, interpretation, the autonomous creation of meaning—could not be achieved by the individual organism. Immediate experience in face-to-face situations is experience of an other, and an external point of view can be imported, enabling one "to look at oneself through the eyes of a fellow man," and so establish the possibility of detachment without which interpretation is impossible. Thus, "social processes are the basis for the detachment that is presupposed in the construction of interpretative schemes 'transcending' the flux of immediate experience."[76] The parallel movement arising from detachment is the creation of a socially defined, "morally relevant biography," that is, a personal past, present and future. Out of the accountability for this that arises in the social situation, conscience is created. Thus, Luckmann can conclude that these processes, which are the means by which the organism transcends its biological nature, and the means to the formation of the self, are "fundamentally religious." They make possible the meaning-systems which relate everyday experience to transcendent values, which allow the creation of symbolic universes.

To the parallels with Hegel already referred to, we can now add the idea of socialization as constitutive of the truly human. We have seen this to be true for Hegel in his understanding of the state as the enabling structure of human freedom, and the community as the context of the religious relationship to absolute Geist. Luckmann believes that it is only theoretically true to talk of an individual "constructing" a universe of meaning along with others, because *de facto* we are born into and inherit a world-view; the accident of birth and the imbibing of the assumptions of this particular world-view in the milk of the mother tongue, lead to the internalization of its assumptions and its adoption as a personal pattern of priorities. And so, "we may now define personal identity as a universal form of individual religiosity."[77] Wherever there is an objective world-view (in every society), there the process of acquiring identity is also the process of expressing religiosity, of co-ordinating everyday experience and transcendent meaning. Similarly, for Hegel, the move from undifferentiated selfhood to a sense of personal identity occurs in the early stages of the achievement of abstract right, which is itself a stage on the way to the ethical. And the ethical, we have seen, rests on the religious. It seems fair to ally Hegel with Luckmann in believing that the processes by which the sheerly biological is transcended are fundamentally religious. It is not quite so clear that Hegel would go along with the relativization of world-views. Once again, his hierarchy conflicts with the objectivity of the sociologist. There is a qualitative difference between Christian world-views, and the pre-and non-Christian alternatives. We shall return to this difference shortly.

Wherever religion is institutionalized in society, and Luckmann sees this as an universal phenomenon, then because "the church is more and less than the 'perfect' historical articulation of a sacred cosmos that represents the hierarchy of meaning in a world-view,"[78] there is a tension between church, sacred cosmos, and the hierarchy of meaning in the world-view, and hence a tension between human identification with the institutional specialization of the church, and identification with the personal value system or hierarchy of meaning. To put it simply, people stop going to church because the institutional form of religion no longer represents their value system; therefore they cannot be said to be exhibiting the decline of religion, and we can only talk of secularization in a carefully qualified sense. Here it refers to the displacement of religious commitment or meaning-systems from the institutional specializations, and not the abandonment of that religious commitment or meaning-system. Luckmann asks the question of whether this constitutes a new social form of religion, and his answer is both affirmative and pessimistic. He concludes that there is a consumerism operating among competing sacred universes, replacing an "overarching and transcendent universe of norms."[79] The absence of any obligatory model leads to a privatization of the adherence to a sacred cosmos, and thus this is in itself very unlikely to lead to a new official model. Rather, the sacred status is bestowed on the autonomy of the individual, and the result is a sacred cosmos which operates as a total ideology, but without legitimation.

Luckmann's historical situation gives him a singular advantage over Hegel in laying out the map of institutional defects and ossification. However, we have already seen that Hegel spoke out against the weakening of religion in his "discordant note" at the conclusion of the lectures on religion. There, he recognized the wandering off of church leadership, and a subsequent divorce between religion and reason, and it is probably fair to see this as at one with his other attacks on subjectivism or emotionalism in contemporary theological thinking.[80] For Hegel, speculative philosophy was truer to theology than theology itself had become, because it provided a measure of intellectual spine for the cultural reality of religion. It is not unreasonable, therefore, to suggest that the religion Hegel was criticizing, if it did not accept the solution he proposed, was destined to become progressively unreal for the great mass of people. And it is fairly evident that it did not accept his solution. The nineteenth century church's options of a non-rational pietism or a romantic liberalism, opposed by an increasingly sceptical historicism and agnosticism, represented the choice of religion *or* philosophy. The former did not seek shelter with the latter, and the latter failed to recognize its roots in the former. It is interesting to note in passing that the single most consistent attempt to stiffen religion with philosophical reason since the time of Hegel is the transcendental Thomism of Karl Rahner, which like Hegelian thought is powered by the idea of incarnation.

We have already noted that the biggest difference between Hegel and Luckmann is in the latter's professional indifference to the content of this or that religious system, as opposed to Hegel's avowed Christianity. The religion which is a permanent feature in Hegel's world is only that which is informed by the Incarnation. Luckmann searches for a functional definition of religion and finds it in the anthropological conditions for the social objectivation of a symbolic universe. These conditions occur in the transcending of biology by the human organism in its meeting with the other. Now this seems to be exactly what Hegel suggests in his study of objective Geist. The arrival at an attitude of *Recht* through the stages of property and contract is exactly this process of coming to humanity. We can recall Hegel's belief that property is the origin of personality, and that personality is first achieved in the recognition of the other as other.[81] And we need to remember that this whole development of *Recht, Moralität* and *Sittlichkeit* culminates for Hegel not in religion but in the state. But the state, like religion, brings the individual into contact with the truth of things. The state is the community through which the individual comes to perfect freedom and so to the perfection of humanity. Within and ideally identical with the state-community is the religious community, which expresses the recognition of the vertical relationship, that between the individual and absolute Geist, which has made possible the absolute validity of the horizontal relationship to the state. The horizontal relationship to the community, and the vertical relationship to God, are two modes of reference to the same truth.

To express this somewhat differently: the idea of the state is truly instantiated only where it passes from contingent usefulness to absolute validity, only where it is seen to constitute the core of human beings as members of a community. But it can do this only insofar as this absolute validity is consciously recognized in the realm of the state. The state as the ethical substance is not itself conscious, but the individual finite subjects are. They are the self-consciousness of Geist, which we have already seen is their strictly religious relationship to Geist, and in virtue of this they can recognize the idea of the state as *their* ethical substance, and experience a concomitant exigency to actualize this idea. Their religious consciousness, in other words, issues in praxis, and the praxis is the actualization of an anthropological and social reality.

Returning to the comparison with Luckmann, the point is that for Hegel a symbolic universe only truly comes into existence in anything other than an arbitrary way where there is a form of consciousness of absolute being, or where there is talk of unity between God and human being. Thus, we could see Hegel more or less accepting Luckmann's analysis, but being unimpressed with an array of symbolic universes or religious cosmoi. Only one could claim absolute validity, and that would be Christianity. However, we could see Hegel going along with the possibility of a degeneration in the cultural form or institutions of Christianity—he did indeed make exactly that criticism, and see a solution offered in a sense from *beyond* religion, from its speculative transformation. (Sociological theory cannot itself be a speculative transformation because it does not entertain value judgments or faith.) Moreover, Hegel's refuge for religion in philosophy would be a perfect antidote to the consumerism which Luckmann argues has now infected the choice of a symbolic universe. Hegel is saying that there *is* an objective standard and that pure subjectivity is less than human because the subject achieves selfhood only in community, that is, in the realm of objective Geist.

This might now point us beyond Luckmann. He has rightly rejected a decline in church attendance as necessarily implying secularization in a negative sense, but he draws negative conclusions in fact, because without the claim to absolute validity that religion in the institutional sense represents, there is only an individualistic consumerism and thus a total ideology without legitimation. Luckmann's argument about the modern world is cogent by and large, and fits the facts. But Hegel's point is that this need not happen, because one form of religious institution expresses the truth of anthropological structures in representational form, and issues in a theoretical understanding of the relation between religion and anthropology which could correct the institutional form without falling into individual consumerism. This corrective depends upon the peculiarly Hegelian form of secularization.

Chapter IV

CHRISTIANITY
AND SECULARIZATION

M any studies of secularization[1] agree in defining the term
as in some way implying a new or increased valuation of
the world. However, the greatest weight is modern studies
of secularization, especially in the more consciously sociological
ones, is given to the idea that the freedom the world wins is won
from something else, and in this case, from the church or from
religion. Thomas Luckmann began by alerting us to the tendency
among sociologists to identify religion and religious institutions.[2] Obviously, if we agree with Luckmann that the truly religious impulse is
to be found in the anthropological structures preceding and leading
to socialization, then any autonomy the world may have wrested from
the rule of the church is not necessarily taken from religion. Even if
we do not agree with Luckmann, however, we do not have to be forced
to conclude that secularization is a process which ends with the death
of religion and the full autonomy of human being. It could be more a
matter of admitting religion and world to their proper and individual
spheres. In any case, the *religious* naiveté of many commentators on
the phenomenon should make us wary of falling in too quickly with
their conclusions, even with the notion that secularization is a clearly
definable process or event at all.[3]

In the introduction, we said that the major concern of this work was
to seek a religio-philosophical justification of the claim that praxis is
the realm of salvation. Such a project has inevitably involved us in
considering the relationship of God and the world. Indeed, we chose

Hegel's state as our theological fixed point because it occupies a formal position in human socialization *and* the divine life, and thus the relationship of divine and human may be made visible at this intersection.

For some theologies, the God-world relationship is simply not a problem. Chief among these are all forms of biblical literalism and fundamentalism, and any view which refuses to pursue the conceptual content and limitations of given religious symbols. An example of the latter might be popular Catholicism, where the vigour of the symbols is shadowed by the danger of idolatry. In both traditions, in fact, God's being *tends* to be looked upon, however unconsciously, as a being among other beings, however much greater. The infinite God is Hegel's "bad" infinite. The infinite which does not somehow incorporate the finite, with which the finite has no real relationship, is reduced to finitude itself. The *saeculum* is excluded from God, although God may intervene in it from time to time, or may expect finite creatures to *earn* salvation within it. Their success will be their promotion to another place, to God's place (heaven), which is somehow opposite to and alien from the world.

Other theological outlooks, of course, press the claims of the secular. Obviously, the options of fundamentalism or popular Catholicism of the form described above cannot appeal for very long to human beings who feel inclined to value either their own lives or those of their fellows in the world, as *something of value in themselves*. Secularization, we might say, is the religious justification of the world; a theology of the world is an attempt to reflect on the phenomenon of secularization, and since it ends by being a justification of the human impulse to value human being and the human world, perhaps we could coin a new term and call it a *cosmodicy*.

The two major theological options which take account of secularization in a positive sense are the broadly dialectical and the broadly incarnational. These two labels are obviously provisional and inaccurate. Nevertheless, they reflect the former's inclination to divide God and world,[4] establishing the world as entirely autonomous, "of age," and the latter's leaning towards a unity of God and world symbolized in the Incarnation. Needless to say, *in practice* the dialectical tendency does not make a total divide between God and world—the human being must live in the world as a believer—and the incarnational does not become a mere identity-philosophy, collapsing God and world. I propose to proceed by engaging in a critical examination of the former, and a defence of the latter, which is, of course, the version closer to Hegelian systematics. But before advancing to that, I wish to make use of Edward Schillebeeckx's useful distinction between the *phenomenon* and the *interpretation* of secularization, to clarify a few of the issues.[5]

For Schillebeeckx, secularization is "the natural consequence of the discovery and the gradual widening of man's rational sphere of understanding."[6] Charting this progress, he claims to identify four turning-points in history: the thirteenth century recognition of a structure of human nature with its own natural law, which humanized morality and therefore interiorized it, and the establishment of the legitimacy of the rational sphere of understanding; secondly, Bellarmine's theory of pure nature, which argued for the first time that human beings have both "a supernatural destiny, and a destiny within the world"; thirdly the fideism of the Reformation, which "left the world, as world, in its full secularity," and created a world-view in which "the verticality of the newly flourishing spiritual life, the Christian witness of the Reformation, came to stand at right angles to the horizontal level of secular life in the world"; and finally, the completion of the divorce of God from rational understanding in the Kantian doctrine that "the objective reality of God could be neither proved nor refuted by 'pure reason'."[7]

Obviously, Schillebeeckx's argument is not dependent on his four turning-points, but rather on the general thesis that secularization is a phenomenon of the coming-to-be of the autonomy of rationality. However, there is a point at which a distinctly positive development—the recognition of the value of human rationality—develops a negative shadow. This seems to me to be an accident of history, and not an inevitability. Human rationality as an autonomous faculty had to wrest its dignity from a previously existing religious system. Every success in the name of rationality was an encroachment on the *status quo*, a challenge to religion. And clearly, the final challenge to religion would be to argue that human reason could know and deal with the living God, because it would remove from religion the last piece of territory it had been able to call its own. The response of fideism is a classic form of protection for God's own domain, as well as a shelter for human beings who understandably find it hard to face the naked reality of a radical autonomy of the secular.

Schillebeeckx believes that the pure phenomenon of secularization is a positive thing. The destruction of the hold over the human psyche of the sociocultural phenomenon of religion makes it possible for faith to emerge more clearly as what it is apart from such trappings. In this respect, Gogarten's position would be in total agreement with that of Schillebeeckx; the difference would remain in their situating faith differently vis-a-vis this secular reality.

It is quite another matter, however, when we turn to the question of the interpretation of the phenomenon of secularization. According to Schillebeeckx, the move from sociocultural religion to Christian faith, because it is a move, we might say, from the seen to the unseen, from the acceptance of the past to the expectation of the future, from speech to silence, is too often interpreted negatively as the end of God and religion. The result is that secularization achieves the status of an ideology, and the secular world becomes a myth of incontrovertible proportions. In fact, he says, "religious sociologists who have studied the whole phenomenon quite impartially . . . say only this—that the change that is taking place in society today shows aspects of secularization."[8] As we saw, Thomas Luckmann came to similar conclusions.[9] And the same argument is presented in an enormously influential article by David Martin:

> Since there is no unitary process of secularization, one cannot talk in a unitary way about the causes of secularization. The whole concept appears as a tool of counter-religious ideologies which identify the "real" element in religion for polemical purposes and then arbitrarily relate it to the notion of a unitary and irreversible process, partly for the aesthetic satisfactions found in such notions, and partly as a psychological boost to the movements with which they are associated.[10]

Martin's article proceeds to discuss the use made of the concept by optimistic rationalism, Marxism, and existentialism. It will be more instructive for us, however, to look briefly at how the secularization myth and its attendant inadequate concept of God has sometimes created havoc even within the theologian's own camp.

God-concepts

A popular example of our problem might be the way in which Bishop John Robinson's *Honest to God* became a world best-seller in the early 1960's. Christians in large numbers were relieved and delighted to discover that the old man with the white beard who lived in the clouds was not an "article of faith," while exasperated atheists and even more troubled agnostics wrote stormy letters to the press.[11] Or, at the other extreme, look at the efforts of British theologians and biblical scholars to "re-interpret" the Incarnation, again in a fairly popular format, this time in the latter half of the 1970's.[12] More often than not, these discussions so set up the question, with human beings "here" and a God "over there" who is as much *a* being as any of us, that the doctrine of the Incarnation comes to seem arrant non-sense. The one question simply not asked, is what the belief in who Jesus Christ was might teach us about the nature of the Christian God.

A more substantial example would be Hans Jonas' attack on the way in which theologians have been seduced by Heidegger to equate "Being" and "God."[13] Jonas quotes Heidegger to the effect that theology is secondary thinking, since it has an object, i.e., God.[14] But this objectification of God might be exactly the problem. Jonas goes on:

> It must be clearly and unambiguously understood that the "Being" of Heidegger is, *with* the ontological difference, inside the bracket with which theology must bracket-in the totality of the created world. The Being whose fate Heidegger ponders is the quintessence of this world, it is *saeculum*. Against this, theology should guard the radical transcendence of God, whose voice comes not out of Being, but breaks into the kingdom of Being from without.[15]

Broadly speaking, Jonas' point is that those who follow Heidegger are falling unwittingly into atheism. But Jonas himself is accepting one very narrow understanding of the relation of world and divine reality — the infinite qualitative distinction of Kierkegaard. The question is begged at the point of understanding the nature of God.

Similar patterns exist in relation to Hegel; that is, Hegel can be accused of atheism if we fail to achieve a sufficiently subtle understanding of what "God" means. In chapter two we saw something of the early critique of Hegel offered by Feuerbach and Marx. Their attitude took the form of a claim that Hegel did not realize how atheistic he was, and Hegel himself found it necessary to protect his work from the accusation of pantheism.[16] Among twentieth-century critics, we could cite Karl Löwith's argument that Hegel's project involved "degrading sacred history to the level of secular history and exalting the latter to the level of the first—Christianity in terms of a self-sufficient Logos absorbing the will of God into the spirit of the world and the spirits of the nations, the *Weltgeist* and the *Volkgeister*."[17] Löwith developed his attitudes to Hegel's God more fully in another place,[18] concluding that the speculative transformation of the Christian and biblical God is "not itself Christian," but rather a post-Christian philosophy. The essential presupposition of the attack on Hegel is the rejection of the extension of the human rational process to the object of religion, God. Fundamentally, it depends again on the objectification of God as *a* being, on the other side of a rationally impassable gulf. The most sensitive and respectful, yet trenchant critique along these lines is that of Karl Barth.[19]

Barth's chapter on Hegel in his history of Protestant theology is a defence of attending to Hegel. Barth praises him first for avoiding the Enlightenment trap of dehistoricising religion in favour of "timeless rational truth." Hegel's argument for the essential identity of philosophy and religion is an attempt to re-establish the medieval unity of human and divine, and here Hegel makes healthy demands on both human culture and theology.

Modern cultural awareness is challenged by Hegel in three directions, says Barth. It is called to see that behind its activity is a search for truth, and it is reminded that truth is the name of God. Barth quotes the lectures on religion: "Reason is the place of the spirit where God reveals self to human being."[20] Secondly, Hegel points out that truth and attendant knowledge is a movement, it has a history. All scientific method and investigation depends on truth and truth on God. That is, science is subservient to the structure and method of knowing. And thirdly, contradiction is the law of truth in history; the absoluteness of Geist is precisely that it is that principle—reason—which relativizes all contradictions.

Barth argues that all this may have seemed a little much for modern cultural understanding to have swallowed. He calls it "a theological invasion of menacing proportion," and says that Hegel had really demanded that the modern human being should found philosophy upon theology, and eventually allow philosophy to be transformed into theology. This, incidentally, is Barth's reading of Hegel's identity of content in philosophy and religion. He clearly sees that the speculative transformation of religion into philosophy is essentially a theological activity. Of course, as we shall see, Barth could not be entirely happy with this state of things.

The second portion of Hegel's demand was directed at theology. Barth first praises Hegel, and points out that theology ought to have had the sense to learn from him that it is not "verbal music-making" but a search for truth; that its truth is discovered always in actuality and not otherwise; and that it should have sheltered under Hegel's giant synthesis rather than the frail umbrella of scientific rationalism prevalent in the second half of the nineteenth century. But Barth's final word is that Hegel's demand may be unacceptable to theology for some good reasons, and once again he names three. Firstly, Barth believes Hegel is wrong to make truth the centre of human being: "Does not man always exist at the invisible intersection of his thinking and willing?" asks Barth. "Is a theory of truth which builds itself up upon the inner logic of a thought which is divorced from practice still the theory of man as he really is, the theory of his truth?"[21] Because of Hegel's consistent emphasis on truth, says Barth, he oversteps the test of human practice: he incorporates sin rather than standing uncomprehending before it, and he treats reconciliation not as an incomprehensible new beginning, but as "a continuation of the one eventual course of truth."[22] Secondly, Barth argues that Hegel treats reason as as much a part of revelation as is the imagination — thus the speculative transformation of the *Vorstellung* is equally divine truth. This leads Barth to a claim which may remind us of Feuerbach and Bruno Bauer:

Hegel's living God . . . is actually the living man. Insofar as this living man is only after all thinking man, and this abstractly thinking man might be a man who is merely thought, and not a real man at all, it is possible that this living God, too, Hegel's God, is a merely thinking and merely thought God, before whom real man would stand as before an idol, or as before a nothing.[23]

Finally, Barth suggests that the identification of God with the dialectical method makes God "at least his own prisoner," and that thereby the divine sovereignty is lost. Because God's self-comprehension is achieved through human understanding, then the whole of God is revealed and lies open to the human knower as God's "own necessity." Creation, reconciliation and the church are all necessary, and "I am necessary to God."

> That is the basis of Hegel's confidence in God and the reason why this confidence can immediately and without further ado be understood as self-confidence as well, and why it did thus understand itself. Hegel, in making the dialectical method of logic the essential nature of God, made impossible the knowledge of the actual dialectic of grace, which has its foundation in the freedom of God. Upon the basis of this dialectic the attempt to speak of a necessity to which God himself is supposed to be subject would be radically impossible.[24]

I have no quarrel with Barth's conclusions from his own premises. It does in fact seem to me that the interesting question that emerges from all this is not whether or not Hegel was as wrong as he is made out to be, but how he could claim to be a Lutheran and say the things he did. Barth is quite correct to see Hegel making truth the centre of human being. He is accurate in his view that Hegel treats reason as a part of revelation, and thus sees an intrinsic relationship between the living God and the living human being. And it is true that for Hegel God is somehow dependent on creation, bound to revelation and reconciliation, and reduced in omnipotence and sovereignty. The conclusion that Barth is drawn to, that all this is somehow a contradiction of Christianity, is not one with which we need feel forced to agree.

There is little to be achieved by polemicising about theological attitudes. Rather, therefore, than make some gratuitous attack on Barth, I prefer simply to point out that there is a quite venerable theological tradition which would make truth (and for that matter, goodness and beauty) central to an understanding of what is *human* about human beings. It is obviously a tradition which depends upon a theology of creation, since thereby what God makes is good and true and beautiful, bearing the marks of the maker. This same theological tradition cannot make some absolute divide between reason and revelation, since revelation must itself be rational if it is to command the assent of human beings and, perhaps even more so, if it is uttered through human agents and interpreted by human preachers. And this same theological tradition, at least in one major variant, would argue that God is dependent on creation, if only to reveal the divine nature *to* that creation.

It seems to me that only an insufficiently thorough meditation on the implications of incarnation can lead one to dismiss this option as not Christian, Barth discusses the "dialectic of grace," but what about a dialectic of the Incarnation, which would itself lead inexorably to a dialectic of God?[25] My claim, then, is that secularization as autonomy feeds upon and strengthens in its turn the concept of God as the *totally* unknown, out there, beyond the great divide. To make this a little clearer, I propose to examine the argument of Tillich's essay on "The Two Types of a Philosophy of Religion."[26] I am convinced that Tillich offers us a more mature understanding of the nature of the essentially religious impulse than is at work in most criticisms of Hegel's religion, even one as sensitive as Barth's.

Tillich's project is to distinguish clearly the ontological from the cosmological varieties of the philosophy of religion, and to show how the latter, unless it depends on and builds on the former, drives a wedge between finite and infinite. The first step is to distinguish Christianity as a whole from the magical:

> The atheistic terminology of mysticism is striking. It leads beyond God to the unconditioned, transcending any fixation of the divine as an object. But we have the same feeling of the inadequacy of all limiting names for God in non-mystical religion. Genuine religion without an element of atheism cannot be imagined. It is not by chance that not only Socrates, but also the Jews and the early Christians were persecuted as atheists. For those who adhered to the powers, they were atheists.[27]

What, then, are these "powers"? They are those "half religious-half magical, half divine-half demonic, half superhuman-half subhuman, half abstract-half concrete beings who are the genuine material of the mythos."[28] The conquering of the powers came about in two ways, in philosophy through their subjection to a universal principle, being, and in religion by their dominance by the God of the prophets of

Israel. This, of course, leaves the question of the relation between the absolute God and the universal philosophical principle. Surely *Deus* and *esse* cannot be unconnected? The two types of philosophy of religion, even the two basic religious attitudes, grow from the answer to this. On the one hand, the equation can be made between *Deus* and *esse*; thus, Augustine proposed that the two coincide in the nature of truth. This insight is at the root of transcendental thinking (and that of Hegel) such that, as Tillich puts it, "God is the presupposition of the question of God."[29] On the other hand, the movement from world to God, opposed to the ontological argument and so making use of the doctrine of analogy, in some way driving an ultimately unbridgeable gap between humanity and God, starts in Tillich's opinion with Aquinas, and amounts to asserting that the structure of reality or reality itself as we perceive it is not *esse*, but the constitution of the human mind. Tillich's most graphic way of expressing the contrast shows clearly why Hegel must stand in the former camp:

> One can distinguish two ways of approaching God: the way of overcoming estrangement and the way of meeting a stranger. In the first way man discovers himself when he discovers God, he discovers something that is identical with himself although it transcends him infinitely, something from which he is estranged, but from which he never has been and never can be separated. In the second way, man meets a stranger when he meets God. The meeting is accidental. Essentially, they do not belong to one another. They become friends on a tentative basis. But there is no certainty about the stranger man has met. He may disappear, and only probable statements can be made about his nature.[30]

There can really be no argument about where to place Hegel. His view of the finite-infinite relationship is so close to that expressed here, namely, that the finite is infinitely transcended by an infinite with which at the same time it is in implicit union. Tillich rightly includes the idealists among those in the ontological camp, but his brief dismissal of their contribution seems directed more at pantheists like Schelling than at Hegel:

Obviously, German idealism belongs to the ontological type of philosophy of religion. It was not wrong in re-establishing the prius of subject and object, but it was wrong to derive from the Absolute the whole of contingent contents, an attempt from which the Franciscans were protected by their religious positivism. This overstepping of the limits of the ontological approach has discredited it in Protestantism, while the same mistake of the neo-scholastic ontologists has discredited it in Catholicism.[31]

Quentin Lauer has suggested that Hegel should be included among the transcendentalists.[32] Tillich would, I think, be in substantial agreement with this. The dialectical "is" and "is not" of the mystics is close to Hegel's own view:

In terms of our ideas of stranger and estrangement, Meister Eckhart says: "There is between God and the soul neither strangeness nor remoteness, therefore the soul is not only equal with God but it is . . . the same that he is." This is, of course, a paradoxical statement, as Eckhart and all mystics knew; for in order to state the identity an element of non-identity must be presupposed. This proved to be the dynamic and critical point in the ontological approach.[33]

In Hegel, we could say that what is represented in religious experience as identity or unity is the experience of the moment of unity in the dialectic. In any case, Tillich claims this as the "dynamic and critical point" for the basis of the ontological argument for the existence of God. The ontological argument is "the rational description of the relation of our mind to Being as such." It is, in other words, the positing of the transcendentals of human knowing as the absolute "in which the difference between knowing and known is not actual."[34] Hegel would express this in terms of the logical Idea coming to be recognized as logically and ontologically prior to finite Geist. The knowledge of the possibility of the absolute Idea as the self-consciousness of reason lies in the rational appropriation of the logic of the divine Idea. The *knowledge of* its actualization comes to us in Christianity. The *knowledge that* it is actualized occurs fully only in the standpoint of speculative thought. Thus, in Tillich's version the move from finite spirit to God by a process of deduction (cosmological and teleological arguments) is dependent on the form and act of God as logically prior (ontological argument). No deductive argument works without making use of processes of deduction and reasoning which, in their use, presuppose a grounding in an unconditioned reason or absolute. You cannot use your mind without implying a form of the ontological argument. "*Deus est esse*, and the certainty of God is identical with the certainty of Being itself: God is the presupposition of the question of God."[35]

The charge of atheism or rationalism, laid against Hegel so often, whether by a Feuerbach, a Marx or even a Barth, comes from thinkers who, whatever their differences, do not recognize the Christian God in the unconditioned of transcendental philosophy. They may be concerned, as a consequence, either to eliminate the deity in favour of secular salvation, or to establish the Christian God on what to them is a firmer, probably more obviously biblical footing. Of the former, more atheistic variety, we have already said enough. But the Christian opponents of Hegel, whether biblical fundamentalists or dialectical theologians, can, as we have already suggested above, be taken together as ultimately non-incarnationalist in emphasis. The positive doctrine of God at work here is that of the Kierkegaardian great divide between the divine and the human. The idea of the absolute which this outlook settles upon is divorced in its essence from human knowing, and divorced from philosophy, which is now not the science of Being but the science of the human mind. With the rejection of the ontological argument, we are left with a God who is posited as one form of existence (the unique case of essence-existence), and creation, which has another form of existence. In this second existence, through philosophy we can seek to establish that God is, and prove it after a manner, but with no confidence. Tillich quotes Gilson:

> It is indeed contestable that in God essence and existence are identical. But this is true of the existence in which God subsists eternally in Himself; not of the existence to which our finite mind can rise when, by demonstration, it established that God is.[36]

As Tillich rightly points out, on this second level of existence we are talking of God's essence as if it were that of "a stone or a star," and such talk is the root of atheism.

Perhaps, then, accusations of atheism against Hegel might be matched by counter-accusations. Hegel's "atheism," if we grant his argument that his system is not pantheistic, amounts to his positing a relation of partial dependence between infinite and finite, and the claim for "implicit unity." His opponents may just as surely inspire a form of atheism by anthropomorphizing God in talking on a human level about that which, in essence, nothing at all can be said. It is the objectification of God which allows for the easy denial of the reality.

The Autonomy of the Secular

There are, as we noted earlier in the chapter, two possible understandings of secularization which can be described, broadly, as positive. Certainly, both claim that Christianity logically leads to secularization. The first of these theories I wish to examine more closely is that of Friedrich Gogarten, who thinks along Lutheran lines, and exhibits an almost total dependence on the Pauline canon within the canon.[37] Gogarten takes justification by faith to be a vertical relationship of the individual believer with God, and the one who is so justified is thereby freed to be responsible in the world. The world is the ambit of works and the law, and secular human responsibility consists in applying the Pauline precept that "everything is lawful, but not everything is helpful." Human autonomy carries the charge to select the helpful from among the lawful.

The faith relationship, says Gogarten, is one of sonship. This provides the context within which the particular responsibilities of everyday are undertaken, but it neither gives advice about what those responsibilities are, nor furnishes the power to carry them out.[38] The individual must do what is good and acceptable judged by the human mind, and do it in faith.[39] So, "Faith, in order to be pure, hands over to man's reason the decision whether or not his deeds are helpful," and "in doing so, it guards man's works in its earthly meaning and from the claim to realize salvation on [man's] own terms." Gogarten's position is at pains to protect God's gratuitous gift of salvation and the divine transcendence.

The world is not to be saved, he goes on, because it is not fallen. A belief in a fallen world is "gnosticism." Only the human individuals can be evil, by falling away from their radical dependence as "sons" or by failing to act responsibly in the *saeculum* as "sons." "Sonship" carries the two connotations of dependence, since one can only be a son (or daughter) in terms of an originally dependent relation to a father or mother, and freedom and responsibility, since the natural dynamism of the child is to move towards its own autonomy. So, sin is always and only an offence against God. The sinfulness is not, it seems, that act, but the implications of the destruction or the damaging of the bond of sonship which the act illustrates. Secular responsibility is a process of "ignorant questioning" about the world, which never gives up the search for wholeness (which would be to accept nihilism) or thinks, on the other hand, that it has arrived at the answer (which would be to make religion an ideology or to canonize some particular "doctrine of salvation"). Christian faith, rather, should live with the openness to the question, and the belief that the answer is expressed somehow in the divine justification of the human being, but without being able to articulate that answer.

The Christian faith is paralleled in Gogarten's view by "Christianity," by which he means a form of Christian living in the world which either ignores or forgets the faith element:

> Christianity, whether understood in general historical or in theological terms, claims that the affirmations of the Christian faith concerning salvation are the answer to that ignorant questioning. It is convinced to possess in this answer the divine revelation of salvation for man and the world. In this way, however, it fundamentally changes faith.[40]

Christianity, Gogarten says, destroys true Christian faith when it attempts an answer to the "how" of salvation; it gives it a content when it should leave it as the *Dass*. By doing this, it does not leave God free to create the future, it does not leave the future open to God, but it interprets the future in terms of possibilities derived from the past and the present.[41] This "Christian secularism" produces the worst form of utopia, "because it completely obscures the Christian faith and makes it inaccessible."[42]

Christianity does have a purpose, however, in Gogarten's view of things. His final picture is of the two held in balance, with Christianity understood positively as Christian life in the world, accepting the Christian faith as its "basis and authority." The most important implication of this is in the recognition of "Christian ethics" as one aspect of secularization. That is to say, no one ethical system follows from faith, because the faith is in a sense contentless. Ethical activity in the world is one aspect of human secular autonomy, to be instructed by "what is good and acceptable guided by the human mind." Gogarten concludes:

> The question for Christian ethics today is whether it will return to secularity, whether it will accept again the appropriate stance of questioning ignorance regarding the whole of human existence, whether it will expose itself again to the future. Only in this way can it recover the counterpart in which, as we say, ethics does not need to be abandoned, because it is a phenomenon of secularization resulting from the Christian faith. On the contrary, here is the legitimate place for reason and for the decision assigned to it, through which man in his historicity cares for his existence. Where this function is fulfilled, faith can retain the appropriate realm in which it remains faith.[43]

Gogarten's version of secularization, and indeed his version of the Christian religion, are the extreme polar opposite of the incarnational variety. But it has been objected to from surprising directions, and for essentially the reasons that the incarnationalists themselves might select. As long ago as 1921, Ernst Troeltsch responded to a polemical speech at the Eisenach colloquium with an article on the relation of Gogarten and Kierkegaard.[44] Troeltsch argues that both Kierkegaard and Gogarten were distinguishing between a wholly personal and private Christianity of the absolute or either-or or "genuine" variety, and the Christianity of the churches, confessions and creeds, and the various historical forms. Certainly, Gogarten's distinction between Christianity and Christian faith seems to correspond to the Kierkegaardian divide between his position and that of "Christendom." Troeltsch continues:

> The encounter with the Absolute, its radical contrast to the world, the self-indictment of man in the absolute situation, and the disregard of all mediation between God and the world, which according to Kierkegaard is the essential interest and work of all churches—that is

the Christianity of absoluteness or either-or, of genuineness and depth of soul, of historical reality and of the idea.[45]

Troeltsch goes on to argue, rightly enough, that even the radical either-or of Jesus or Luther had a content, or at least implied a content. Jesus' decision was for the coming kingdom, which "could then provide the positive content of religion and its relation to the world," and Luther's "new man . . . had to work out his relationships to the 'world'."[46]

Of course, Gogarten's reaction against the Christianity which merely accommodates itself to the world is both understandable and justifiable, says Troeltsch, characterizing Gogarten's "absoluteness" as "radical Christian dualism." Troeltsch's response is more intuitive and emotional than it is intellectual, by his own admission, and he describes it in contrast as "a wholly instinctive and naive concept of religious dualism." For Troeltsch, however far beyond human logical processes is God's activity of creating, it is not opposed to the world, but carries the world within it. Troeltsch's affinity to Hegel is very clear here:

> God's being and continuous creative activity . . . are themselves the life of the world, constantly dividing themselves to become finite life in its fullness and to raise the finite out of self-love and self-glorification to union with God and service to him; they are themselves constant self-repudiation and constant self-incorporation.[47]

The revolutionary conversion that they demand of the individual, therefore, "grows out of the inner depth of his being and is already latent in his love of self and of the world." This is "the most profound revelation of God," and the primary task is then to give appropriate historical shape to this revolution within each "period and each living man." Troeltsch concludes that this position as he has outlined it may not be the essence of Christianity, or even "still" Christian, but that it is "essentially Christian" in the sense that it "stems from Christianity." He adds: "I must characterize Gogarten's position as intellectually impossible for me."[48]

There are no essential differences between Gogarten's position as Troeltsch criticized it in 1921 and the later version we have discussed. In any case, the Troeltschian critique of Gogarten is entirely accurate.

It is clear that Gogarten is working with too narrow a canvas of the New Testament—essentially nothing more than the Pauline argument on justification in the Letter to the Romans. His divorce of God from the world leaves no scope for a theology of praxis, let alone for considering a view of salvation that takes praxis to be its matrix. His attitude to faith is entirely individualistic, and takes no account of how the human subject to whom the faith is to reside, is a being moulded and influenced in a thousand ways by other human beings. Faith in Gogarten's view is exclusive rather than universalistic, and consequently so would be his attitude to salvation. Of course, there are good things about his position; in particular, the need to protect Christianity from complete subordination to the cultural assumptions of this or any other moment. But that protection should be for nothing other than Christianity's critical and educative function *vis-a-vis* the world. His most perceptive point is surely that of the need to leave God free and the future open, and not to build a secular utopian future which is nothing other than the imposition of the past and present thought-models on the yet-to-come. But as we shall shortly see, that does not involve us in abandoning a sense of the value of the world or its intrinsic connection with faith.

Probably the most trenchant contemporary critique of Gogarten, at least in English, comes from Larry Shiner.[49] Shiner sees three different but related processes at work in Gogarten's secularization: the desacralization of the world, so that even the written law is reduced to a "worldly phenomenon;" the separation through the notion of sonship of the worlds of faith and work, through which secularization is the counterpart of faith; and the autonomy of reason within the world, at the expense of openness to the mystery of the world.[50] Shiner's critique makes many of the points we have already considered, but he adds several "tasks for theology" which he sees growing out of his critical but appreciative reading of Gogarten. In the first place, he feels that if faith is somehow to delimit the boundaries of desacralization, then there must be something in the openness to divine mystery that suggests *this* direction rather than *that*, and that the task is not to identify principles but to "distinguish the Gestalt of the faith-attitude from its opposite":

The discovery of forms of community that do protect and enhance man's existence as a person would still be a matter of reason and in that sense secular. But it would be an ethical reflection that proceeded from a phenomenological analysis of the structure of the human personhood that becomes possible in faith.[51]

The second task, consequent upon this, is to identify the ways in which receptivity to the divine mystery affects our actions towards others. Task number three is "to find a concept of reality that can account for the continuity of nature and history," since Shiner sees Gogarten arguing that God is the creator of human historicity but not of nature, and so that human beings are deeply dualistic. Shiner's conclusion would stand well as the statement of our task in the next part of this chapter:

> Thus, the most fundamental task of a theology of secularization is to place the conceptual analysis of the twofold responsibility of man before God and for the world into a coherent intellectual context. What is required here — as in the case of the nature-history problem — is an ontology that can put each dimension of being and rationality appropriate to it in its place without creating a closed system. The aim of such an effort would be to illuminate both the distinctiveness and the interconnection of nature and history, of being and action, and to show their relation to the reality of God as it is known in the subjectivity of faith.[52]

Secularization and Incarnation

Writing in 1968, Schillebeeckx saw the crisis in both Roman Catholic and Protestant thought as the result of fideism, which he described as the cleavage of human experience and Christian faith. Gogarten's position certainly makes a virtue of that cleavage. Catholic theology has a time-honoured tradition of valuing the human, especially human reason, in at least the preliminaries for theologizing, but it may be that the tension in Catholic theology between the admission of reason to a role in thinking about God, and the concept of the magisterium as a hierarchical teaching authority which hands down decisions about the content of "the faith," is the Catholic form of the "cleavage."

If indeed we can take what Edward Farley has characterized as the "collapse of the house of authority"[53] as a fact, which may be more questionable in the Catholic tradition than in those where the scripture principle has held sway, (perhaps for no other reason than that the magisterium has more big guns with which to fight back than the unpersonified principle can master), then it is more trite than tendentious to state as an axiom that theology may not bow to anything but human reason and human experience. Theology can be described as a reflection on experience in the light of tradition, a reflection, moreover, which is validated only in its faithfulness to that tradition and its adequacy to the experience upon which it reflects. This is not to claim, of course, that the human reasoning and reflecting process never reaches a limit, which limit we could name "mystery," but that the limit is something acceded to at the end of the theologizing process, not something setting pre-ordained limits. This kind of reasoning Hegel implied in his attack on what he saw as emotionalism in theology, and in his consequent insistence that philosophy was being more faithful to the data than was theology itself. Hegel always claimed that his thinking was based on experience, and it could be argued that looking long and hard at the phenomenon of religion was the true core of his insight into reality.

The problem with Gogarten's views, which we have admitted to the discussion as one serious estimation of secularization, one way of giving value to the secular, is that they are not truly open to human reason. At one and the same time, they seem irrational, and are built on a principle which excludes by definition the incursions of reason. Reason belongs in the *saeculum*, and may not intrude upon faith. The faith conviction is not touched by rationality; indeed, the non-rationality of the faith conviction is precisely that which gives autonomy in its own world to reason. The two kingdoms of faith and works / reason may never meet, and only the former has anything to do with salvation. The problem with this, of course, as Shiner pointed out, is that human beings exist both in the world of nature and that of spirit, and that therefore the dualism to which this position subjects them, leaves literally no single concept of the human as a thing of value. There is value in the human relationship in faith with the justifying God, but there is no value, as such, in human works in the world. This is why Gogarten can say that sin is something which only has to do with God. For Gogarten, the sinfulness of these "wrong" human acts is not in the act itself, but in the fact that it is a transgression against the relationship of "sonship" established in God's justifying grace. It seems to me possible that we may want to demand a more adequate explanation of wrongdoing and human responsibility to other human beings. And how would Gogarten's position speak to the modern phenomena of "structural sin" and "institutionalized violence," or the sinfulness of nation against nation?

If there is an alternative vision of the value of the saeculum in Christianity, then its superiority to the Lutheran model has to be found in its more thoroughgoing consistency and adequacy both to human experience and to the Christian revelation. In seeking this second way, we shall take as our point of departure that which the Christ-event as a whole testifies to, which is a certain understanding of incarnation, and in this we shall be in the spirit if not the letter of the Hegelian synthesis.[54]

The cross and resurrection are constitutive or founding events in the faith-affirmation of the individual or community. Taken together in some way with the events of the life of Jesus of Nazareth as available to us, they lead to some form of the faith-claim that "Jesus is Lord." The Christian faith, in other words, is intrinsically connected with a claim about who Jesus Christ is. To concentrate upon the cross, or indeed the resurrection, to the exclusion of turning these events back upon a question about the being of the person to whom they in some sense happened, is to settle for the level of acts rather than being. And an act-soteriology is essentially magical, whether a soteriology of redemptive suffering, or some other version. On such a model, there is no way of explaining the mechanics of salvation without being forced to have recourse to an anthropomorphizing conception of the deity, and *settling finally for that level*. But to take the further step with the logic of the faith-affirmation and ask the question of the identity of this person carries us in principle at least beyond anthropomorphism and beyond magic.

Faith, then, is not so much faith in an act of God as faith in the revelation of Jesus Christ—the revelation that exists in the total life, death and glorification by God, not faith in this or that event or word or deed of Jesus of Nazareth. In the same way, the revelation in which we are invited to believe is not a propositional revelation, but the revelation of the nature of the relationship that God has with us which Jesus Christ *is*. That is, he is the revelation and he is the type of the relationship.

What do we know for sure about the historical individual which it seems we must posit as in some sense behind the Christian belief? Perhaps we know only that he was a human being, and nothing more. Without that human being, we are not dealing with anything at all outside our own minds. Then, in the process of the faith affirmation, we also "know" that that human being is a revelation of the divine reality. Again, without this second stage, we are left with a magic, act-soteriology. When we bring the two pieces of knowledge or the two convictions together, we have something which stands in the classical Chalcedonian tradition of incarnation. We affirm the full humanity and divinity, and we make no attempt to hide the contradiction in which we seem to be involved.

We can, however, say a little more. We can certainly say, in particular, that if Jesus Christ is a revelation of God, then that in Jesus Christ which makes the revelation of God possible in a human being, is something which we share with him in virtue of sharing the same human nature. Only if he is not human is it impossible to say this, and if he is not human, then the conviction of salvation through this "x" cannot be sustained. This capacity for being a revelation of God must then be something which is not contradictory to the state of being human. This principle seems to me to be vital, since it gets us away once and for all from the blind alleys of "infinite qualitative distinction" and "radical sinfulness." The former makes it impossible to present any revelation of God in the world, and the latter makes it impossible for such a revelation to inhere in a human being—saving, once again, the magical or anthropomorphic versions of reality.

We might call this, with suitable modesty, a phenomenology of the faith-affirmation of a rational being. To say "Jesus is Lord" and not to abdicate the full humanity of one who says this, leads inexorably to the conclusion that the human and the divine are not adequately explained if they are declared to be total opposites. All this is in line with the Hegelian principles that what is important about the Incarnation is the *idea* of the Incarnation, although that idea does not achieve full actuality until it has been instantiated in a single human individual; that the true infinite is not totally other than the finite, but overreaches it; and indeed that finite Geist is a moment in the divine life, and that as an agent of the self-knowledge of the infinite, absolute Geist, is truly a necessary moment.

If such an approach leads us to a less magical interpretation of salvation, it also offers us a chance to make a little more sense of the doctrine of grace. For Gogarten, justification by faith is a free and unmerited act of God, by which the sinner is saved. Clearly, salvation is God's gift, and we have no reason to quarrel with the gratuitous nature of that gift. To suggest simply that a human being can earn salvation is to propose a model in which the finite controls the infinite. But the problem with Gogarten's view is that it then becomes a matter of *whom* God chooses to justify, and the implication is that there may well be some or even many whom God chooses not to justify. So we move from the freedom of God to the caprice of God, from a quality which we can predicate of an infinite and unknown, to one which nourishes the anthropomorphic illusion. If, however, we identify grace tentatively with what we have already called the capacity for the divine, then it is no less the free gift of God, since we are dealing with a creator God (although Gogarten may not be), but it takes the less-than-human quality of caprice out of God's "psyche," so to speak, and places responsibility for salvation firmly in human hands. What God freely gives is human nature as something not intrinsically sinful, and in the revelation that is Jesus Christ, the possibility of a faith in the essential trustworthiness of God's free bestowal of that relationship is made available. With Rahner,[55] we could say that grace is an anthropological structure; the peculiarity of this structure is that with it we are also given the freedom to fail to utilize or develop this capacity for the infinite. And, clearly, the responsibility here falls more heavily on those who have been offered the chance to express their faith in the revelation that this is so, in Jesus Christ. But it does not mean that the gift of salvation is not given to the rest of the human race, simply that the faith in the trustworthiness of the revelation of that gift is precluded, at least in full explicitness. To put it in more Lutheran terms, we could say that justification is given in creation, and revealed in the free identification of God with the justified creation in and through the event of

Jesus Christ. The faith, then, is in the revelation, and to those to whom the faith is offered, the faith justifies by being a faith in the trustworthiness of the revelation that we are justified—that is, that we do stand free to be at one with God precisely as human beings. As for those to whom this faith is not available, for whatever reason, it does not mean that they do not stand justified, since that justification is part of human nature, but simply that the possibility of explicit response to that gift is precluded—and precluded not by a capricious choice of God, but by the force of created circumstance.[56]

This representation of an incarnationalist position may seem at once too individualistic, and too faith-oriented at the expense of works, and thus to fall into at least some of the pitfalls of which we have previously accused Gogarten. The demonstration that this is not so will take the form of a few comments on the theology of secularization implied in this incarnationalist position.

The picture so far deals with a holistic conception of human being. There is no justification for separating a vertical faith-dimension from the human being's other activities and capacities occurring at the horizontal level, still less for investing the former with the whole of ultimate meaning and value. The whole human being is involved in any and every dimension of human life, including that of faith. The response in faith, then, to the revelation offered in Jesus Christ, is a response of the whole human being. The ability to respond, which we have called grace as the capacity for the divine, is a structure of human nature. But if this is the operative structure in the faith-response, it is not the only structure at work. Everything which goes to make the human being is involved in the act of faith, including the cultural and historical situation of the individual within a particular community. Everything which makes the human being truly human either comes from or is activated by the phenomenon of intersubjectivity. The individual is the product of the interaction of faculties and relationships, and it is this complex process of becoming human which stands behind the human faith-affirmation. If the response to the offer of faith in Jesus Christ is to be a full response, it must be the response of the full human being. A purely emotional attachment which does not lead to intellectual conversion is as nugatory as a purely intellectual response which has no visible outward signs in the emotional life and the lived choices of the person concerned.

Further, a full human being is one who lives a human life in the world in a thoroughgoing intersubjective involvement with other human beings. We can agree with Gogarten about the role of human reason in choosing to live humanly, make truly human choices and moral decisions, and all the other aspects of the pain and the joy that make up human life. Where we differ is in insisting that these choices and activities are instrumental in creating and recreating the particular person who responds in faith. We do not respond as human being, but as this or that human being. In this sense, we might say that works have a prior role to faith, because works, broadly understood, make me *this* or *that* person.

We have already argued that the faith-affirmation is a response to the revelation of the essential or implicit unity of the human and the divine. The revelation in Jesus Christ is above all a revelation of the value of the human and thus of the world as a whole; the Incarnation is God's valuation of creation at the same time as it is God's free subjection to that creation. This revelation is then the divine seal upon the truly human; essentially, indicating as it does the true continuity of the human and the divine, it establishes the autonomy of the secular as the activity of the sacred. If affirms the sense in which human beings are the divine agency in the world, and by doing this it of course gives in its turn a new and awesome dignity to works. In this sense, faith leads to works. Faith in the revelation of Jesus Christ establishes the secular as a truly sacred realm, because the revelation is a revelation of their continuity. And with this, the truly human is revealed as the form of divine activity in the world.

This leaves us with a circular and mutually strengthening process. The works of the fully human being give depth to the faith-affirmation. Indeed, they may be said to make possible the recognition of the depth of the revelation, because they provide for a fuller understanding of the truly human which is given value in the revelation. And the faith-affirmation in its turn strengthens the conviction that this world of works is "God's work." Moreover, any understanding of faith which drives a wedge between faith and works is essentially self-contradictory, since faith is so closely bound up with the divine valuation of the truly human.

Such a theology of secularization is diametrically opposed to the Lutheran model; it is based on a radically non-dualistic vision in which the human is a moment in the divine, and therefore in which everything that happens to and through human beings is at one and the same time secular and sacred. The secular is the objective moment, we might say with Hegel, of the sacred. Further, by establishing that the fully human is the context of faith, it opens the way for a theology of praxis. It is left for the human sciences to determine what the fully human is, prior to or apart from the faith-affirmation. But *that* that fully human is at work in faith is the determination of theology. And if the revelation in Jesus Christ is the revelation of the divine involvement with the fully human, then when, as now, the human sciences have established intersubjectivity and corporate responsibility as existentials of modern human being, the way is open for a political theology. In fact, to be faithful to twentieth-century human being, it may be that theology must be political theology.

Chapter V

POLITICS AS SALVATION

I n the previous chapter, we established what could be called a theology of the world. It is in that world that the views expressed in this current chapter must be taken to claim validity; in Gogarten's world, they would be a nonsense. Here we shall build upon all the elements that have preceded this chapter, and shall try to show the relevance of the Hegelian philosophy of the state to political theology. It will be recalled that in our discussion of Hegel's state in chapter two, we dealt with it from three points of view: the relation of objective to absolute Geist; the relation of the state to its constituent individuals; and the relation of state and history. In seeking now to apply Hegel's ideas in an explicitly theological context, there three aspects reappear in slightly different guises. We shall first consider the notion of praxis in political theologies, and make use of the Hegelian dialectic of individual and state to throw light upon the possibility of non-ideological praxis. Then, the question of the relation of objective and absolute Geist will again come into play as we discuss the dialectic of kingdom and world. Finally, we shall turn to the question of responsibility, or the dialectic of Christian commitment to one's own society and the claims of justice in a wider world-order.

Praxis:
The Dialectic of Individual and Community

As we noted briefly in the introduction, one of the cardinal points of Latin American liberation theology is the primacy of liberative praxis over theology. To put it in the words of Gustavo Gutierrez, "Theology comes after."[1] The reason proposed for making this axiomatic is that theology, like other theoretical activities, cannot but be influenced by the ideological presuppositions of the theologian. Indeed, "ideological suspicion" is one of the keys to the methodology of political theology in general, and theology of liberation in particular.[2] Juan Luis Segundo explains that the phrase means "that anything and everything involving ideas, including theology, is intimately bound up with the existing social situation in at least an unconscious way."[3] The radical exercise of ideological suspicion carries as far as the scriptures, where "exegetical suspicion" operates on the assumption that the interpretation of the Bible, and even the redaction of the different books, has been subject to ideological forces. This particular claim lies behind the liberation theologians' predilection for yet another new search for the historical Jesus; they hope thus to uncover a pre-ideological layer and circumvent the abstract Christ and the equally abstract Spirit.[4]

Clearly, we need to question the possibility of unideological praxis. The picture the Latin American theologian presents is of a prereflective option for the oppressed, and the expression of this in liberative praxis with and on behalf of these oppressed. This prereflective identification or solidarity is obviously much more feasible in a society where the oppressed represent the vast majority of the populace, where the gap between oppressed and oppressor leaves no room for doubt, and where the level of vested socioeconomic interest and the absence even of relatively democratic social structures offer no viable alternative. But it does not make it possible to avoid the question whether such a prereflective option can be unideological. One of the major points of the notion of ideological suspicion is that ideological presuppositions can and do operate sometimes at a deeply subconscious level. But more importantly, it is difficult to see how without at least an implicit theory of society, liberative praxis can be liberative, because without this theory there can be no effective *direction* to praxis. An *ad hoc* response to individual injustices may lead to a fairly inchoate revolutionary consciousness, but what is that as a force for change without an ideal or a utopian vision to move towards? And can there truly be such a vision without its being in some way ideological?

Now let us turn and look at the same problem from the perspective of the more theoretical European political theology. Dorothee Soelle's definition of political theology, which we quoted in the introduction, draws a contrast between ontological or existentialist points of view, and the political sphere. She says little more about the ontological, but contrasts the individualistic bias of existentialist pre-understanding (*my* life) with that of political theology, with its wider social basis (authentic life *for all*). Soelle considers that the presupposition of political theology is that society is in principle transformable, that the major tool in this transformation is not demythologization but ideological criticism, and that through this tool the kerygma will be freed from ideological overlay for creative interaction with political praxis.[5]

Several remarks must be made at this point. In the first place, the presupposition that society is in principle transformable must, it would seem, be required to furnish some sort of justification for itself, particularly since the facts of human existence would tend to support the opposite point of view. Moreover, we can ask the same as we asked of the Latin Americans: transformed into what? Surely we need some idea or final cause that is going to govern the direction of the social transformation. And will this direction itself not be susceptible to the overriding tool of ideological criticism? Or is there some non-ideological idea available? Again, Soelle calls for the use of ideological criticism to uncover the kerygma. But if the kerygma is freed in this manner, what will it then be? Historical consciousness has come to recognize that nothing can be expressed outside of some historical context or other, and that the prejudices of the interpreter are in fact constitutive of understanding. Must not ideological criticism conclude that its exercise is merely the replacement of an unreflectively ideological interpreter by one who is aware of the role of ideology?

The question we are asking, then, is whether there can be some vision of society which escapes the charge of ideology; this is one issue raised in liberation theology and posed in a different way by the work of Dorothee Soelle. In looking for an answer, I want to go back to the option that Soelle dismissed without further reference, that of an ontological point of view. For it does seem to me that Hegel's notion of ethical substance offers an ontological framework for the construction of a political ideal, and thus a direction to liberative praxis, which is not easily dismissable as ideologically motivated.

Political theology's challenge to traditional theological approaches is that ontology without praxis is mere abstractionism. But praxis without ontology is chaotic. We could sketch a number of possible models for the relationship of praxis and ontology, and the one which is insupportable is exactly the one which political theologians (rightly) fear—praxis given its place within a fundamentally ontological framework. What we must search out, rather, is a reciprocity between praxis and ontology, and we shall find it by concentrating our attention upon human subjectivity.

Let us recall the major features of finite Geist's role *vis-a-vis* ethical substance, the Hegelian state.[6] Above all else, we have to remember that the actuality of the ethical substance resides in the relation between the individuals and the idea. The true Hegelian community does not come about by accident, or pre-exist the human subjects. They must create it, and recreate it, constantly, in seeking to draw the reality of their particular social situation into conformity with the idea of perfect community. So the state is actual when it concretizes freedom, and the freedom about which we are talking is the freedom of the human individual to be truly himself or herself. This is why we can be so apparently glib about a "perfect community." When the state as perfect community exists, and only when it exists in that way, can the freedom of the individuals and the freedom of the community be exactly equivalent. This utopian vision demands not only structures which will allow this freedom to be instantiated (Hegel had his structures for his day, and there is nothing sacrosanct about those; only the intention, not the particular structures, transcends the times). It also requires a vision of what the freedom would be like. Moreover, since the freedom about which Hegel talks is a freedom to be fully human, the vision of that towards which the individuals must strive, indeed, the idea of the state itself, needs to be couched in anthropological terms. The ontology that we seek in Hegel's vision is an ontological anthropology.

Among the many phrases Hegel used to describe the state, a particularly revealing one is "Geist objectified."[7] Hegel's God is absolute truth, perfect reason; thus, wherever structures which are rational exist in human history, there there is truth, and there the divine is objectified. To say that the state is Geist objectified is exactly similar to saying that the state is the "absolutely rational,"[8] another favoured formulation. At the same time, individual human beings are for Hegel "finite Geist," which is to say that they are the same truth and reason in a further form—differing both from rational structures and from God, and yet the same insofar as they are in truth and acting according to their nature as rational. As we have seen at some length above, this status for human beings is dictated by the progression of Geist to mediated presence to self—human beings are the moment of its alienation. And as we further saw, this entire process only escapes the charge of being a vast and unsustainable hypothesis with the introduction of the idea of incarnation, and faith in its having occurred in the life and death of Jesus of Nazareth. Hegelian anthropology and ontology are totally interdependent and mutually dependent upon a christology which, since it is the basis of effective knowledge of the power and nature of finite Geist, is itself a soteriology. And such a soteriology is totally identical with the instantiation of the anthropology.

Human beings, who exist always in community, strive towards the fuller concrete freedom of that community, as the context in which they can be most fully themselves, and so in their turn be most free. In different times and places the means by which this end is sought may vary considerably; what is important is that every step they take is a truthful, rational one, since every step is both a means towards a society in which that nature can be more freely expressed, that is, to a more rational society, and an end, as an expression of the concrete freedom which resides in that human nature here and now. A faith in the Incarnation makes this difference, and perhaps only this difference: it is the divine benediction upon the truth of human nature, or, if we wish to express it differently, it is the confirmation that the truth and reason of human nature is identical with divine truth and reason—with "the nature of things."

The dialectic of individual and community, then, is really a struggle between human selfishness and the truth of human nature as a being in community. Or it may be the tension between the rationality and truthfulness of the human being's drive towards a community of justice, and the communal selfishness of civil society. In the perfect community, such a struggle would cease, because the perfect community would be a community of perfect individuals. Here lies the role of "liberative praxis."

The subject's liberative praxis takes place in the context of a community. In this more or less concretely free community, the praxis is oriented towards greater concrete freedom. The means to that vary from time to time and place to place, saving only that praxis must not only be directed towards concrete freedom as the instantiation of reason, but must be an act or series of acts which expresses reason and freedom. (This, in passing, is what makes violence so difficult to justify.) Here too lies the possibility of prereflective liberative praxis. Because liberative praxis is an expression of what it also is directed towards, that is, concrete freedom of the individual within the community, it does not take assent to the theoretical position to make possible the practical application. The practical application is simply the expression of human nature. The theory is the recognition of this particular ontological anthropology.

So, is *this* understanding of liberative praxis truly non-ideological? Have we found a position that can be safe from ideological suspicion? We can answer affirmatively, on one condition, namely, that the core of the kerygma which Dorothee Soelle thought ideological criticism would uncover is that human nature has the potential for being the expression in history of absolute truth, freedom and justice, and that the fact of the Incarnation is the symbolic expression of the kerygma. The kerygma, behind everything that has accrued to it over the centuries, or that was in the mind-sets of the early redactors and communities, must be the figure, albeit shadowy, of the human Jesus of Nazareth. Reflection upon the full and evident humanity of this man must lead to a claim about the nature and possibilities of human nature. If *this* insight into human nature and its absoluteness can be the kerygma, and not anything else, then all that we have said above can follow without major problems. However, the moment we seek to give a specific content to what this nature of Jesus was like, we become more tentative, although not necessarily wrong, and we become open to ideology critique. Thus, curiously enough, we can base our faith not upon some attempted access to the historical Jesus, but exactly upon the faith of the early community—not its faith in this or that phrase, miracle, or act of Jesus of Nazareth, but its faith in the absolute validity of the human perfection of this man—expressed in their terms in their times.

Where does all this leave our political theology? In the end, it leaves us where adults in a "world-come-of-age" must be, which is only to say that it leaves us where the God of freedom would wish—with a religious justification for putting our faith in human reason. This human reason must carry us towards an ideal which involves bringing ourselves and everyone towards full humanity, and which is brought about by expressing our full humanity. The gospel offers no solutions, still less any favoured political structures. It simply establishes the divine mandate for human truth and rationality. It also offers the supreme example of concrete human freedom, and tells a warning tale of what happens to the person who engages in the dialectic of individual and community. Salvation lies in the exercise of our full human natures, and liberative praxis is just such exercise. Since this liberative praxis must amount to political activity, it brings us neatly back to Dorothee Soelle's claim that "politics is understood as the comprehensive and decisive sphere in which Christian truth should become praxis."

Political theology has to be a formal or philosophical activity. What it constructs is the theological justification for the importance of the *polis*—which, as we have seen, is accomplished through a theological anthropology which hands responsibility to human beings. This theological anthropology also lays down the principles by which the political theology must be conducted: the primacy of human reason, and the insistence that the end to be achieved (perfect community) can only be arrived at by means which are to be installed in their fullness only in that end. The end of a world of human freedom in reason and truth is only possible if those same values are exercised in its creation. Or, to put it a little more biblically, the kingdom is within us, and it is with us now. Salvation is now. Clearly, the eschatological model of this point of view is the "already/not yet" of the Pauline reservation. And this, of course, is precisely the pattern suggested by all Hegel's concern for the end of history. As we have said above, the end of history has arrived in the sense that the speculative philosopher's achievement has been to bring the ideas with which the world can be understood into human consciousness.

Hegel's vast synthesis is really a hymn to the transcendental role of human reason, and it is this which lifts political theology out of being empty, if well-intentioned, theorizing. Political activity is its own justification. But political theology is the provision of the direction without which that activity never gets beyond treating the symptoms of the sickness.

The Dialectic of Kingdom and World

Since theologians of liberation make a great deal of the historical Jesus, and of the liberator God of the Exodus, they not unnaturally concentrate upon Jesus' inauguration of and call to the kingdom. The question that always has to be asked, though, is just what the difference is between the kingdom and the world. What is the kingdom in its fullness, and how does it differ both from the world as we have it now and the world as we would wish it to be? Where is the kingdom in our world, and what is the difference between the kingdom of God and a political utopia?

When Jesus began to preach that the reign of God was at hand, the content of that message was not revolutionary. "What the kingdom consisted in could not be a problem for any reader of the Old Testament."[9] It was not the content of the kingdom, but its timing that was the message:

> When Jesus said that the kingdom of God was at hand and behaved in such a way as to force the irruption of the future, he was simply thinking and behaving in the tradition of the messianic humanism of the Old Testament.[10]

This argument is taken further by Jon Sobrino. His interpretation of Marks' gospel is that Jesus' proclamation of the kingdom had to go through serious revision after the crisis at Caesarea Philippi; that is, his early proclamation of the kingdom was, in a sense, *too* orthodox and traditional.[11]

Be this as it may, the point illustrated here is the familiar one that there is little if anything new in the content of Jesus' proclamation. It is the fact, the forcefulness and the authority with which the proclamation is made that accounts for its impact.[12] And, of course, this derives directly from the identity of the proclaimer, felt perhaps at the time, but understood only in reflection on the events of death and resurrection.

The Old Testament conception of the kingdom, proclaimed anew by Jesus, is one of a society of perfect justice, where "all will be just."[13] Miranda, who goes to great lengths to delineate the characteristics of the reign of God, seems to me incontrovertible in referring us in summary to Psalm 146:

> He who does justice to the oppressed
> He who gives food to the hungry,
> Yahweh is he who gives liberty to prisoners,
> Yahweh is he who restores sight to the blind,
> Yahweh straightens those who are bent over,
> Yahweh loves the just,
> Yahweh protects the stranger,
> He who sustains the orphan and widow,
> He who frustrates the unjust,
> Yahweh reigns forever.[14]

The most consistent theologizing of this act of Jesus in proclaiming anew the Old Testament vision of the reign of God occurs in Sobrino's work. Sobrino distinguishes two strands in Jesus' preaching about God: the sapiential tradition, stressing the goodness, providence and patience of God, and response of the faithful; and secondly, the prophetic-apocalyptic tradition, the love and judgment of God which renews reality and calls forth a renewal from the people. This latter is more important in Sobrino's opinion, and has its force in the way in which:

> Jesus' preaching about God is always framed in the context of his proclamation about the kingdom of God. . . . The essential reality of God is inseparably bound up with the operative reality of the reign of God.[15]

In the Old Testament, Sobrino goes on, God exists in so far as God acts, and "in Jesus' view, God 'is' or 'exists' insofar as he creates community and human solidarity." We come to God then, through some human mediation:

Our filiation vis-à-vis God is necessarily mediated through brotherhood between human beings. Without the brotherhood, the filiation is wholly and purely idealistic. Brotherhood is not just an ethical consequence deriving from a God already constituted and known; it is the very way in which God really is the Father, and in that sense, God. In Jesus' eyes, a God who does not create brotherhood simply is not God at all.[16]

Sobrino establishes a picture of Jesus following the Old Testament understanding that the acts of God are the being of God, and that these acts centre upon the creation of community and human solidarity. We come to God, moreover, through our sharing in this human fellowship. This pattern can be exactly paralleled in the following manner: Geist comes to its fullness by passing through the moment of alienation in its actualization in human history, to the reintegration of that alienated Geist into the absolute. God must posit the other of God (finite Geist and world), and insofar as the conscious part of that other becomes aware of its true nature (in speculative appropriation of religious truth), it will seek the fullness of its nature (the perfect community or state). Indeed the conscious participation of finite Geist in this process is the means by which Geist comes to its fullest self-possession. This conscious participation is another form of reference to praxis. State, then, is both a human and a divine perfection — it is perfect community, and it is the fullest instantiation of divine truth possible in the structures of human history. No other conclusion of our investigations into the meaning of secularity could have arisen. (Again, at the risk of being tiresome, we must insist that the Hegelian state is the ideal of the perfect community, and states are states only insofar as they actually instantiate this ideal.)

Do we then have to say that kingdom and world are identical? Not exactly, although we may *want* to say that kingdom and state are identical. World is a fact, and it is not more or less world in virtue of its conformity or not to the speculative truth of the Hegelian vision. World is that which Geist works upon, so to speak, in growing towards its fuller realization. World is that in which state and kingdom strive to come into their own. Although they may be identical, there is a difference between the Hegelian state and the kingdom of God as the Old Testament understands it. As I hope we have by now satisfactorily established, state is a formal reality—it depends for its existence on the honesty and clarity of different ages and generations, in seeking to actualize concrete freedom according to their particular conceptions of it. The Athenian state, the Prussian state of Hegel's time, and the modern democracy all have elements of the Hegelian state in them, but none of them is its apotheosis. The Old Testament kingdom is one specific vision of the state—the vision which derives from an ancient theocracy. It is formally correct in that it seeks to establish the characteristics of the kingdom from the nature of its God. And, of course, the predication of certain human attributes of its God is a direct consequence of what it considers to be vitally and radically human. The danger of projection here will only finally be overcome with explicit faith in the Incarnation.

In the language of the times, the Old Testament conception of the reign of God represents correctly what Hegel means by the state. And, of course, if Hegel is true to his expressed purpose in distilling the representative truth of religion into the conceptualizations of philosophy, that is exactly what we should expect. But if we go on from here to make the claim that the state *is* the kingdom, are we not reducing eschatology to a political utopia? That is to say, whatever claims we make for the Hegelian state, it remains an idea bound for its actualization to human history. The only absolute correlate of the state, so to speak, is undifferentiated Geist; the state is simply the shape that reason takes when it is expressed as the structures of human historical communality. If we represent Jesus' proclamation of the kingdom as exactly equivalent to Hegel's delineation of his political philosophy, are we not involved in some measure of reductionism?

There is a sense in which we cannot avoid arguing a lack of equivalence between state and kingdom, and it has to do with the notion of religion. The idea of the state is not a replacement for religion, but the historical "horizontal" correlate of religious reference. Human beings, born into and living in community, reflect on their faith in the incarnate Lord. They derive from this faith a firmer grasp on what they bring to this faith, namely, a conviction that solidarity or community is the shape of the Christian life—this is the message of revelation and the mode in which salvation is communally expressed and individually discovered. And the implications of their faith thus direct them to the future building of that community whose idea is that of "the state." Hegel does not summon us to religion, but to an understanding of the relationship between Christianity and the moral life. Jesus calls to action, and in this sense the liberation theologians are closer to him than they are to the speculative philosopher. The philosopher only claims an understanding of that action which Jesus demands.

At the same time, there is a further sense in which state is equivalent to kingdom. Hegelian speculative philosophy is oriented essentially to the past: Christian action to the future. Yet both have their being only in the world of the present. And the vision of the state has grown out of the appropriation of past events, as the proclamation of action on behalf of the kingdom would be impossible without some conceptualization of the kingdom, to help select what is or is not the *appropriate* action. The past events to which the idea of the state relates were calls to action, like Jesus' proclamation of the kingdom. Hegel's idea of the state is the speculative transformation of the *Vorstellung* of kingdom. Kingdom knows the truth, but does not know that it is the truth. Kingdom is the prereflective expression of the perfect community conceptualized in the idea of the state.

Neither kingdom nor state, then, exists as perfectly actual. But in any given present moment, both are actual as the presence of meaning. State is the recapitulation of what has been and its speculative expression in an idea; but this idea has within it potential. Conceptually, it is complete, but the indicative leads to the imperative. For Hegel, philosophy must stop at the indicative. Kingdom, on the other hand, is the expressed potential for action that the idea of the state preserves formally. Kingdom is the dimension of hope that orients the present towards actualizing the idea.

The "now" towards which state and kingdom each relates is the world — the neutral face of human events, the other of God. Its return to God begins with the appearance of reason in that present — "the rose in the cross of the present," as Hegel refers to it.[17] And this reason, which we have seen can in terms of the structures of human sociality be referred to as "state," imposes a direction upon the present. Meaning is conceptually prior to action, if action is to have direction: but action is chronologically prior to meaning, if meaning is not to be mere abstraction.

This relationship suggests a particular understanding of hope. Hope is not mere hopefulness, a vague expectation that God will act in our future. The future only exists in the present; "future" is a cipher for the existence of meaning in the present moment. Christian hope, then, is faith in the existence of meaning in the present, because that present meaning gives direction to action. Future is the imperative that derives from the indicative.

We might wonder how close this is to descriptions of God "calling from the future," or of the "lure of God" beloved of process theology. Such concepts wee understandably developed in reaction to a backward-looking religion, or to a God who was the justification of the *status quo*. But their unsatisfactoriness is that they present God as the *absolute future*, against a traditional theology which sees God as the *eternal present*.[18] Rubem Alves puts this well in criticizing Barth and Moltmann:

> For Barth the future is formally and actually already ahead of us. The historical events in the present, therefore, do not mediate a new future. The future is not born out of the present. On the contrary, the now and man's freedom acquire their significance when they are an imitation of, and play under the light of, the future that is revealed to man. Moltmann attempted to correct this, but he still affirms that the future, although not ontologically, is formally ready and as such moves the present by attraction towards itself. For both of them, however, the present does not mediate the future.[19]

Alves' objection to the Moltmann variant is biblically based; the biblical communities "did not know a God whose essential nature was the future, the *primum movens* ahead of history." God is rather "the presence of the future" and, along with Sobrino, Alves concentrates on the acts of God, which "created a present in which the future was being formed."[20]

But it is not only from the experience of the biblical communities that we can criticize this conception. In effect, if the God of the future is now somehow in the present, then the shape of the future is unknown and indeterminate. If God exists as promise, of what is this promise a promise? Without an answer to that, once again, action towards the fulfillment of that promise is directionless. The purely future eschatology, even on the sophisticated lines of Moltmann, is a form of the magical or anthropomorphic. It settles for the symbol, and does not allow it to give rise to thought.

The persistent tendency to read Hegel as negating or rejecting the value of the future is well-illustrated in Louis Althusser's interpretation of temporality in Hegel:

> Since time itself directs us to the *concept* as its essence, i.e., since Hegel consciously proclaims that historical time is merely the reflection in the continuity of time of the internal essence of the historical totality incarnating a moment of the development of the concept (in this case, the Idea), we have Hegel's authority for thinking that historical time merely reflects the essence of the social totality of which it is the existence.[21]

Althusser isolates two characteristics of Hegelian historical time, its "homogeneous continuity" and its "contemporaneity." These correspond roughly to what we have earlier referred to as the chronological and ontological dialectics. The former is the time-continuum as that in which the development of the Idea is manifest. The latter is implied by the former; that is, it is the possibility of seeing the structure of the "social totality" in any one moment of time by taking what Althusser calls an "essential section":

> This section is only possible because of the peculiar nature of the unity of this totality, a "spiritual unity," if we can express in this way the type of unity possessed by an expressive totality, i.e., a totality all of whose parts are so many "total parts," each expressing the social totality that contains them, because each in itself contains in the immediate form of its expression the essence of the totality itself.[22]

Thus the continuity of time is possible "as the phenomenon of the concept's continuity of presence with its positive determinations." The Hegelian moment is a moment of "a development," and a moment of "the presence of the concept with itself in all its concrete determinations." So, says Althusser, nothing can run ahead of its time according to Hegel, for the present is the absolute horizon of all knowing. And so there can be no anticipation of historical time, no anticipation of the future development of the concept, no knowledge of the future.[23]

Althusser's interpretation of time in Hegel is, on the whole, correct. We have already discussed at great length the role of objective Geist as the presence of the absolute in its other—relative, finite, contingent human history. And it is clear that Hegel's work divides into discussions of the logic of the dialectic, and delineations of the dialectic at work in political, aesthetic, military and cultural history. There are, therefore, large areas of complete agreement with Althusser's depiction, although his use of the terminology of essence and existence is a little misleading.

Althusser's point can be made clearer by reference to the priority of knowing over being in the Hegelian schema. What we see taking place in history is not the development of the concept, but the developing knowledge of the concept by finite knowers, and the realization that this is the developing self-knowledge of the concept. Absolute Geist differs from the logical Idea not in its structure, but in the fact that it has become self-aware through a process of alienation from and return to self. What develops in history is the realization on the part of finite Geist that the structure of reality is the conceptual form, and the path to the realization of this is the dialectical struggle of the knower with what is unknown, in the search for greater knowledge. Speculative philosophy achieves its supreme insight in the realization that its activity is the form of reality. But the only development that has taken place here is that through finite Geist's capacity for self-consciousness, logic has itself become self-conscious.

Althusser is of course quite correct to call this a "spiritual" unity. That which each part of the "expressive totality" contains is nothing more nor less than a rational structure; that is, it can be known to be a part of the totality by knowing Geist. As rational, it can be incorporated into the spiritual unity—thus, the irrational or evil is a negation, an irrationality which threatens the spiritual unity. This spiritual unity is exactly what is under consideration in the frequent depiction of the basic religious impulse as a conviction that reality is ultimately meaningful—the inarticulate striving of the human spirit to express its sense of oneness with the whole. In a sense, all Hegel has done is put words to this feeling.

If this explication is correct, then Althusser's complaint about the role of the future in Hegel's thought is misplaced. There can be no anticipation of the future development of the concept, because there is no future development of the concept to be anticipated. The preface to the *Philosophy of Right* puts beyond dispute that Hegel thought "nothing could run ahead of its time." Nothing philosophical, that is, for philosophy only describes. Althusser complains that there can be no political science in Hegel, because there is no possibility of a future prediction from current events. In this he is right; in Hegel there are no future utopias. But because Hegel's philosophical reflection on experience does not attempt to predict, that does not mean that his position is without implications. As we said much earlier, Hegel might very well have wished Marx good luck with his revolutionary objectives. His only caution would be that to seek to change the world is not the role of the philosopher. That is not to say that a philosopher's work may not inspire change; after all, to an extent Hegel inspired Marx.

Both orthodox and political theologians can fall victim to ideology. They can accept an interpretation of the goal of human history, or of the goal of a particular society, and bend their understandings to planning for it. If salvation is afterlife in a specific place (heaven), then the alternative is also a place, and if God wills human beings to be saved, then the whole machinery of sanctions and rewards, and the view of human history as a vale of tears in preparation for eternal beatitude comes into existence. If the mission of the German people was proclaimed as the triumph of the Aryan race, then the implications for Jews and others were clear. But salvation cannot be won through spiritual terrorism, and the political utopia as a community of freedom is only as close as the immediate prospect of free and totally human action. The curiosity and the contribution of political theology at its best is that it is apolitical. It directs the Christian to act *now in the present day* out of purely human considerations. Its underlying anthropology, as we have already seen, must therefore be a vision of perfect humanity as ultimate salvation—since the Savior was perfectly human and simultaneously a presentation of absolute values. Its attitude to coexistent political ideologies, be they Marxist or capitalist or whatever, has therefore to be pragmatic and opportunist. The direction of Christian praxis is decided by its ontological anthropology—the means it uses are whatever it finds to hand which does not contradict that vision of humanity.

This is also the vision upon which Hegel works. As Althusser saw, Hegel is himself in just the same sense apolitical. He looks not to the future utopia which justifies a strategy in the here and now for its eventual accomplishment, but to the present moment, in which the fully human act is all the divine truth that there can be in the world in the only moment that matters—this moment. But, once again, if this is indeed Hegel's way, and if it coincides with the apolitical political theology in its governance of actions by the principles of an incarnational ontological anthropology, then there is a lot to be said about the future which such a conception implies, even if he cannot legitimately talk about it.

Such a vision is demanded of the Christian in any and every society in which he or she may live. Such a vision may make use of any and every political system which does not require actions which would be the self-contradiction of the ontological anthropology, but overall the stance of the Christian towards these political systems will be independent and marked by a criticism with a positive orientation. The hope of the Christian lies not in naiveté or in a utopianism, but in the conviction that with the Incarnation the possibility of acting in concrete, radical freedom has been bestowed on humanity. God is the presence of the future as the present power of acting freely in our full humanity. Thus, where we see that action in our world, we derive great strength and solace from it, and we talk of sanctity and so on—whether in the religious leadership of a Mother Teresa or John XXIII or Oscar Romero, or the prophetic inspiration of a Martin Luther King or Philip Berrigan. But we also see that action less spectacularly wherever we or other human beings act out of our full humanity. This kind of action, and only this, is the justification for the exalted status which Hegel gives to finite Geist in the process of absolute Geist. In any and every moment in which finite Geist strives for the actualization of the ethical substance, the idea of the state is being actualized. In these moments, the kingdom of God is all around us.

Volksgeist and Weltgeist
The Dialectic of State and World

Our late twentieth century world is one in which nations give lip-service to the notion of interdependence, but pursue national interest more and more firmly. Not the least of Hegel's acute premonitions of the world beyond his time was that of the difficulty of forming a "league of nations" such as Kant had suggested:

> This idea presupposes an accord between states; this would rest on moral or religious or other grounds and considerations, but in any case would always depend ultimately on a particular sovereign will and for that reason would remain infected with contingency.[24]

This judgment stems from the Hegelian principle of the sovereignty of the individual states, in virtue of the fact that the state is the actualization of Geist. There can consequently be no "universal will with constitutional powers over them," and international law is as a result a system of treaties which cannot *de facto* bind. Its fundamental proposition has no authority beyond an "ought-to-be": "treaties, as the ground of obligations between states, ought to be kept."[25] This, of course, is a remarkably prescient depiction of the essential weakness of the United Nations; its moral exhortation is heard only where it coincides with the particular interests of member-states.

The practical issue that I wish to raise in this section is that of responsibility. Does Hegel leave room for, or even contribute to our understanding of, a wider involvement in the world than that of building the community of the state? The pressing context of this question is obviously that of concern for the economic crises and growing inequities of our world. I do not hope to provide a glib Hegelian solution to a gigantic world problem. Rather, I would like to see the issue as a variant on our question about the theological significance of praxis. *Ought* nations to deprive themselves for the sake of other nations?[26] To express this question in terms of the state as ethical substance: is its function complete with the perfection of the internal relationships of those constituent finite individuals who together actualize Geist in history, or is there natural progress to a further stage?

In many respects, Hegel seems to stop at the nation. We have just quoted him as saying that beyond the state there is no sovereignty, no moral authority, and it is a notorious though misunderstood fact about Hegel that he believed patriotism and war to have at least a partially positive function. They are the individual's identification with the state.[27] However, the final stage of the Hegelian view is that the state serves a larger whole, and here we shall find the philosophical justification for a wider view of liberative praxis.

In the *Philosophy of Right* the subdivisions of the discussion of the state are "Constitution," "International Law" and "World History." On the Hegelian pattern, these are the opposite poles and their synthesis; "constitution" obviously refers to the structure of the state in itself, and international law to the external relations of the state with other states. The recognition of the existence of other states, which creates the need for international law, obviously raises the matter of the higher point at which these individual states have their common ground. Now, of course, what individual states have in common, at least in principle, is the rational exercise of freedom, which is their *raison d'etre*. Thus, the relation between individual states and world history is exactly parallel to that between individual finite spirits and the state as their ethical substance:

> The principles of the *Volksgeister* are wholly restricted on account of their particularity, for it is in this particularity that, as existent individuals, they have their objective actuality and their self-consciousness. Their deeds and destinies in their reciprocal relation to one another are the dialectic of the finitude of these minds, and out of it arises the universal Geist (*Weltgeist*), the Geist of the world, free from all restrictions, producing itself as that which exercises its right—and its right is the highest right of all—over these finite spirits in the history of the world which is the world's court of judgment.[28]

If we refer back to Louis Althusser's explication of Hegel's understanding of time, we can represent the relationship between the state and universal history as that between the essential section and the historical continuum. In the terminology that I have sought to use, the state is the logical, universal history the chronological dialectic. At any one time, if we look to history itself for the existence of Geist, we shall have to indicate this or that particular state. Hegel himself pointed in particular to the Athenian state, the Roman state, and modern northern European states. He also looked hopefully towards America as the land of the future. It does not so much matter *which* state, as that the existence of Geist in history must be located somewhere, and therefore in some state or other. We cannot point to universal history itself, because it *is* nowhere in particular, except in the states of the time in which we happen to be. Just so, if we are asked to point to the rationality of the state in actuality, we have to point to the activity of its individual human constituents. But the principle towards which these individuals and this state at some particular moment in history in fact are bent is the realization of absolute reason, absolute Geist. They are the presence of absolute Geist in that particular moment in time, insofar as they act out of their free rationality.

We have earlier been at some considerable pains to show that the basis of this free rationality is anthropological. It has its origin in a certain vision of human nature, and it finds rules for its exercise in the faithfulness of human beings to that nature. The implementation of the idea of the state cannot take place, for the simple reason that it is self-contradictory, if it does not occur by the free activity of human beings. The act of the state which does not proceed from the free rationality of the human subjects is *not* an act of the state, *ipso facto*. The principle for relations between nations, which goes beyond their individual sovereignty, is similarly ultimately dependent on the free rationality of the human subjects. Moreover, with speculative philosophy's understanding of the situation, the larger purpose of the state is visible; it serves *Weltgeist* or universal Geist, whose "right is the highest right of all." But the *Weltgeist* is nowhere, except in a people striving to give political expression to its human freedom — *Volksgeist*. When speculative thought sees that this is what is occurring, then the notion of a wider responsibility is born.

Finally, it would seem, we stand on the brink of leaping beyond Hegel. So far we can go; indeed, he offers some sound theoretical principles for the exercise of this responsibility. It would be very easy, for example, to use Hegel to articulate a view that the primary responsibility of the state, *vis-a-vis* other states, is to enter into treaties which would express the ought-to-be of concrete human freedom. Or, to say the same thing in our own terms, relations between states must be governed by the principle that the end towards which the state is directed — concrete human freedom — is also the means by which that end is brought about. This principle would have the most profound consequences for international trade and development. That it does not occur in so equitable a fashion is simply one more piece of evidence, if such should be needed, that individual states are themselves engaged in internal struggle to bring the idea of the state to expression in the context of civil society, which is ever dragging the body politic towards the satisfaction of complex and frequently illusory needs.

But it is just here that the problem arises with Hegel. As individuals in our respective societies, is our duty to the struggle for the realization of the idea of the state, or to other individuals in other societies, struggling more desperately against attacks upon their concrete human freedom? A whole treatise could be written on this point, beginning, not least importantly, with the need not to identify "concrete human freedom" necessarily with the western idea of representative democracy. But the Hegelian problem is that there seems to be no machinery for going beyond the actualization of the state within my own particular society. At any one moment in time, for Hegel, the state is the sovereign authority.

A "reconstruction" of Hegel cannot be accomplished simply by saying that his view was just the reflection of the political consciousness of his times, and that at a time when, for example, Germany was such a new political entity, he could not be expected already to be looking beyond it. It is more important to review once more his central point; if the state exists as the ethical substance within which concrete human freedom is a real possibility, and if that ethical substance is actualized in civil society through the actions of finite individuals, then the role of the Christian in the world is the realization of justice. Again, Hegel would accept that but he might insist that the Christian must do this through the state. There is no ground upon which the individual can act in concrete freedom, outside activity which builds up the state.

Here we have to express qualified disagreement with Hegel. If we are right in our interpretation, then the root of the whole political activity is in an anthropological vision. The common denominator is thus not *polis* nor even nation but human race. He is of course correct in making use of the state, because of the need for structures of human organization as a rational and free community. But if the enabling structure is then identified with the end of the enabled activity, an empty circularity results. And Hegel does not say that; for him, the end of the state is the self-production of universal Geist, which is identical with the free rational activity of finite Geist. The state itself then seems to point to a wider responsibility, so that activity itself in its turn actualizes the end towards which the state must move. To put it more practically: international consciousness and praxis is, even when it does not seem so, a step towards the creation of a community of concrete human freedom in our own society.

Liberative Praxis
A Practical Postscript

Liberative praxis is the wholehearted implementation of the fruits of an anthropology fired by the Incarnation. It is a political theology because it seeks the erection of structures of concrete freedom in the everyday "secular" world. And its vision of the status of the human being and the quality of human action means that the human beings are alone in the world, challenged to bring about their own freedom, which is God's freedom, the freedom of the children of God. The state of freedom is to come about through the process of liberation, because the liberating action is the exercise of that which in the fullness of freedom shall be fully possessed. The free human act in the here and now is proleptic of the fullness of the kingdom.

There is, then, a certain starkness in this view of Christianity. It belongs in a "world-come-of-age," and there is a sense in which it claims that God is dead. God will not come to our aid as something superadded to our own efforts. God is our own efforts, and, much more, all that our efforts could be. Most problems in the world are of our own creation. The vast majority, and certainly all those we have created, are in principle within our power to solve. What holds us back is greed or fear rather than ignorance. The greed and the fear is a lack of faith in human beings, and a consequent inability or refusal to act out of what our vision of human nature requires of us here and now. To implement the vision, it must already be active in what we do and how we do it.

How this particular need to implement the vision looks in different countries and parts of the world may vary considerably. The perspective of Latin American theology of liberation demands radical and sometimes violent political upheaval, alongside the re-creation of the church from the grassroots upwards—the phenomenon of the so-called "Basic Christian Communities."[29] This pattern is the result of a scientific analysis of Latin American society carried out by those who stand in a practical and prereflective commitment to the oppressed of that continent. Their hard experiences and their sociological analysis unite to form a politically radical and articulate righteous anger.

The problem in a different situation is to follow the process from our own perspective without emasculating it. It is too easy to say that we live in democratic societies, and therefore that we should follow our inherited political structures in ordered progress towards even greater justice. We need the same pattern of prereflective commitment and sociopolitical analysis. The former is more difficult for us, because the oppressed of our own societies are more difficult to identify, but the latter may be easier, because we have the relative freedom to conduct it. The problem that this creates, from the perspective of theologians of liberation, is that without the prereflective commitment (which is supposed to circumvent ideology), the analysis cannot but be a reflection of our own presuppositions, be they Marxist or bourgeois capitalist. The solution is not an easy one but it does seem to call for the creation of our own kind of "basic Christian communities," expressing perhaps the more subtle marginalization that takes place in more developed societies, as well as the more insidious forms of oppression, not least the psychological oppression we exercise upon ourselves through the delusions of "anticommunism," "international aid," or "apolitical religion." Analysis of our own societies will certainly lead to unpleasant conclusions when the effects of international trade, development policy, and the wastage of the earth's resources are uncovered. What it is vital to see is that the politicization of the individual and the community which must occur as a result of reflection on the analysis will issue in a platform based upon a vision of the true nature of human being. Political analysis leads to political theology, which in turn leads to action. And, of course, the analysis was in the first place a result of praxis, This is why the first stage must be the promotion of basic Christianity community through which the praxis can be focussed and reflected upon.

Chapter VI

A THEOLOGICAL POSTSCRIPT

In the present work we have been concerned to explain and defend a single thesis, namely, that if we evaluate the incarnational roots of Hegels' notion of the state, we will uncover a basis for a theological vision which can rightly be described both as a Christian anthropology and as a political theology. Hegel's conception of the relation of finite and infinite is real, because actual, within objective Geist, and hence most evident in the permanent human struggle to express the fullness of humanity as freedom in corporate social structures. The state, in the carefully qualified sense in which we have seen Hegel uses the term, is the context of the concrete historical expression of the fullness of human nature. The conscious awareness of human beings that this is the case has come about through speculative reflection on the historical fact and the religious symbol of the Incarnation. Thus, the Incarnation, by revealing finally the true nature of human being and its relation to the absolute, releases the self-conscious exigency to pattern the human world according to concrete structures of human freedom. With faith in the Incarnation as a revelation about human beings as well as about the nature of the divine, religion as the struggle for human liberation is activated.

All that we have said in the foregoing chapters was intended to give this kind of prominence to incarnation and anthropology as the two poles of the theological axis. But it was not intended to suggest that with this accomplished, nothing remained to be done. The theological world could not turn without its axis, but the surface is far bigger and more varied than its northern and southern extremities. Theology has to extend to the whole range of human life and the doings of society, and in this final chapter we shall make a brief circumnavigation of the globe, although there will be time only to call at a few major ports.

The need for this theological journey extends beyond the urge to satisfy the conceit. It has too often been asserted of liberation theology, especially in its earlier days, that its applicability lies only in the less-developed, "non-democratic" countries of the world. It is equally possible to misconceive political theology as a modern form of the social gospel, or as a theology of politics, or as some other partial theological enterprise. In fact, if the approach of this present work is accepted, such limitations of the political must be cast aside. Our brief theological excursion, then, is intended to show that a central political motif such as the one we have adopted can be the basis of a comprehensive theology.

Any theology has at its core a concept of God, of human beings, and of the relation between the two. Of the three, the relation is most significant, since it is the quality of the relation that dictates the extent to which the concept of God can be anything other than mere guesswork. No relationship: no knowledge. In Christian understanding, the term "grace" is frequently if not universally used to refer to the relationship of the divine to the human. The word signifies both the beauty and the gratuitousness of the gift, without being too specific about its essential nature. In seeking its nature, in this book we have been at some pains to find a way between two extreme and often caricatured positions; namely, on the one hand, the theory of God's free and so almost arbitrary act of justification of the sinner, and, on the other, an equally unsubtle understanding of grace as a substance conferred by God on human beings as a reward for the practice of certain rituals or the public avowal of certain beliefs. The former position, we believe, does not make enough of human beings, and the latter makes too much, by suggesting that human rituals can exercise power over the divine.

The relation between God and human beings we are proposing here circumvents this particular issue by rejecting both an anthropomorphic image of God, and the "absolute qualitative distinction" between God and human beings, substituting instead the formal model of the relation of the Hegelian finite and infinite. The finite is a moment in an infinite process. The succession of finite moments is necessary to the infinite process, in the sense that without the finite moments there would be no knowledge of the infinite process beyond immediate and subjective certainty. But no one individual finite moment is in itself essential to the infinite process, although one moment, that of the Incarnation, is essential to the possibility of the finite succession's recognition of its role in the infinite process. Thus God is not dependent on me, although my life is a constituent in the divine process. Conversely, what it is in my life which is constitutive of the divine process is, above all else, reason. By my exercise of reason in my life I am a moment in Geist. It is, therefore, the presence of reason in human life, not the contingent details of that life, upon which reason works, that is the point of divine-human union. And so I am certainly dependent on God, not for every minor and major problem, still less for their solutions, but rather for the power of reason by the exercise of which my life can be transformed into one that is more human.

This model of the divine-human relationship presents human beings with great responsibility. It offers them no material solutions to their problems, and it calls upon trust in their God-given humanity. Just as it represents a departure from the normal understanding of grace, so it implies a similarly unorthodox approach to revelation. Revelation is not contained in a book, and it is neither open nor closed. The book is a record of preliminaries and responses to the revelatory event of the Incarnation. Reflection on the anthropological import of that event releases the trust in human reason and imagination which is the true locus of revelation and the source of future and past insight. So the event initiates faith in the process, and the practice of reason, in which the process consists, stimulates further reflection on the founding event.

Just as we saw in the matter of a theology of grace, so here in the theology of revelation there are two possible extreme positions. On the one hand, it can be argued that revelation is nothing more (and nothing less) than the written record of the Bible, the place where God caused the divine truth to be set down for human beings to consult and obey. On the other hand, it can be argued that the Bible is just one cultural expression of broadly religious belief, and that it is in no way normative for theological reflection. Again, it seems to me that the first position leaves little freedom for human beings, the latter gives them too much. It is quite clear that the scriptural records are a product of human reason and imagination, and a product of God, since God is the creator of these human attributes. Human reason and imagination make possible a divine revelation communicable to human beings, but at the same time they limit. God cannot reveal more than human beings can see. Nevertheless, the record *is* there as a history of the developing understanding of the one principle of reality to which Jews and Christians alike have subscribed. The revelation is a history, a record, and while it is perfectly possible to go off on some other conceptual tack, that which claims to be Christian theology must be that which stands in continuity with this history of this God. That said, the history in the Bible and the subsequent developing understanding cannot fruitfully be distinguished, since they are both functions of God-given human reason and imagination, working within the parameters of a particular religious tradition.

Thirdly, and we have already said much about this, salvation consists in the practical implications of this revealed understanding of grace. Christians have never finally settled for one or other of the various primitive metaphors for God's redemptive act through Jesus, not least because the anthropomorphization of the Christian God runs counter to the essential mystery of the divine in the Christian tradition, and the caprice of such a God contradicts the natural inclinations of plain common sense. Jesus Christ did not redeem by doing something, but by being who he was, and accepting obediently and in trust the fate that being who he was made it inevitable he should suffer. The final significance of the cross and resurrection is that they spark off the conviction that the crucified and risen one is the incarnate Lord, the perfect revelation of the divine-human relation. It is, of course, this relationship which is salvific, and knowledge of it brings conviction of or faith in the salvation. It is when we add the conviction of faith to the anthropological condition of having been saved, that concomitant responsibilities emerge. Foremost among these duties is that of seeking to live a life which expresses the divine-human relationship, that is a *fully* human life. Such a person will seek to realize the state, because it is only in the context of concrete structures of human freedom, corporately, that *full* humanity is possible.

If all this is so, we are now face-to-face with the question of the relationship of salvation to liberation. Salvation we can now see is the anthropological condition of relatedness to the divine as a finite moment of an infinite process, while liberation is the living realization of this in concrete structures of human freedom. The two have therefore their respective priorities, *ordo essendi* and *ordo cognoscendi*. Only the actuality of an absolute significance to the individual human life makes the struggle for social and political freedoms rationally explicable. But only the total human involvement in the cause of freedom and justice engenders the love for human beings as human beings which opens the believer to the efficacy of Jesus Christ's self-giving.

Consequently, it would be a misconception to identify salvation and liberation. The former is a state of affairs, the latter a process, and if an individual is not engaging in the process he or she is in fact in self-contradiction. He or she therefore cannot be said to be behaving in a fully human fashion. True human nature is being contradicted. But at the same time, refusal to accept the implications of full humanity is not *ipso facto* a formal rejection of God's self-revelation. To express this very traditionally, such a refusal is sin but not necessarily damnation.

At the same time, salvation and liberation are obviously closely interwoven. The human being who comes to reflect on the revelation of Christ from the standpoint of liberative praxis achieves a real assent to salvation by accepting the concomitant responsibilities to the state for the fullest possible set of reasons. There can be no doubt that prereflective commitment to liberation is entirely possible, and that Christian faith may or may not result from that commitment. If we stand back and analyze what happens in such a case, then we may say that a person is seeking an absolute grounding to the value of that to which they are already committed, and finding it in the gospel of Jesus Christ. But this is only a theological explanation for what may be expressed equally correctly in the following way: in the struggle for liberation, understood as the struggle to implement concrete structures of human freedom, the committed individual comes to know God.

Where, then, does this leave the person who is engaged in the struggle for liberation but does not achieve faith in the Christian God, or even consciously rejects it? The question returns us to the basic religious impulse. When I seek an explanation for reality and my involvement in it, do I *commit* myself to a human interpretation of the world, or do I *submit* myself to an absolute ground which is greater than the sum total of human judgments, and relativizes them all? If I do the latter, then I am a religious person. If I further argue that the absolute supports a world of human beings to whom, in principle, everything is possible, then I am at least an anonymous Christian. And if I find that absolute uniquely revealed in Jesus Christ, then I am undoubtedly a Christian.

In consequence of this, the non-believer who is yet committed to social liberation is certainly actively expressing his or her state of having been saved. Everyone, of course, is saved, since this is the anthropological condition revealed in Jesus Christ. Similarly, the rejection of salvation is not noetic but existential. That is to say, I reject salvation—I am "damned"—when I live in a way which *in fact* constitutes a contradiction of the divine-human relationship as revealed in Jesus Christ. I am damned, in other words, when I live out a thoroughgoing contradiction of the truth of human nature.

It is the conception of human being as brought to fullness in the context of structures of human freedom, that is, corporately or in community, that makes the religious anthropology into a political theology. By the same token, self-contradiction (damnation, at its extremes) is essentially political. To contradict my essential humanity, and therefore my salvation, it is necessary for me comprehensively to reject the struggle for human liberation. In its fullness, this can only be achieved by being a thoroughly evil human being. To do it from the ranks of conscious Christians, it would be necessary to engage in a systematic denial of the connection between salvation and living a moral life. Few, if any, Christians would want to say that the ranks of "good" and "bad" people bear no relation at all to the ranks of "saved" and "condemned." However, there are many of us, perhaps most of us, who refuse at some time or another to accept the full implications of the relationship between salvation and liberation. And this refusal, it seems, is the fundamental meaning of sin or sinfulness in the political context. My sin is *at one and the same time* a contradiction of my human nature, and so an offence against the creator, *and* an offence against society, and so political. Conversely, of course, anything which truly builds the concrete structures of human freedom cannot be sinful.

There are a number of criticisms which can be levelled against this theological position, and in conclusion I should like to consider three of them. It can be accused of being so secular that the "vertical" dimension of Christian prayer and devotion has disappeared, or at least lost its significance. It could be said that the exaltation of the state removes the need for the Church. And it might be argued that such an optimistic view in such a painful and evil world is sheer blinkered daydreaming.

Prayer and Politics

The state, as an idea to be implemented, is that through which human beings express their natures. But as far as it is implemented in this or that society, it is an objective structure. Prayer, on the other hand, has to do with the subjective disposition of the constituent individuals, even when it occurs in a communitarian or ecclesial context. It is their conscious recognition of the absolute ground of their lives, and it therefore only exists among those whom we have described as taking the broadly religious attitude, be they Christians or not.

In approaching the matter of prayer, however, we are not only distinguishing between those who are religious and those who are not, but also among the religious themselves. Within that company, there will be those who, as Hegel would put it, have the capacity to rise to speculative thinking, and those who cannot. Political theology, like any other intellectual activity, is not to everyone's taste, and such theological complexity should not be expected of all or even most Christians. To put it in more Hegelian fashion still, we could say that most people receive the truth of what is, representationally in the form of religion, and not speculatively in the form of the concept. They are in the truth, without knowing that they are in the truth. Or rather, they have a subjective conviction of the truth (faith) without the objective certainty (knowledge). Prayer, then, is the natural recourse of those who do not achieve objectivity.

To say that prayer is more natural to those who are not inclined to speculative philosophy is not to claim that those in possession of a good working political theology can dispense with prayer entirely. Just as the whole Hegelian philosophical-theological system cannot convince alone, but requires a belief in the Incarnation in Jesus Christ to raise it beyond an elaborate hypothesis, so our theology or philosophy of the state and its construction cannot really command assent without commitment to the vision of human nature upon which it depends, and that, in its turn, as we have shown, is only possible with a firm belief in the actuality of the Incarnation. This belief, of its nature, is not objective, and therefore requires the peculiarly subjective strengthening which prayer brings.

When "prayer" is under discussion, it is often the repetition of vocal prayers or psalms, or the singing of hymns, or the "prayer of petition" for various needs, that is actually being discussed. Some of these are at least apparently forms of prayer which seek to influence God, and consequently suspect of dependence on mythological or anthropomorphic representations of the divine. But whenever it is the classic types of prayer—of praise, adoration, thanksgiving—which are under consideration, they can clearly be seen as forms of more or less directly subjective reference to the mystery of the divine-human relationship. That is to say, they are acts of openness to the truth of the relationship. This is even more apparent when we advert to "private" or "silent" prayer, and it is not without significance that mystical and monastic traditions have tended on the whole towards the belief that the higher the prayer, the fewer the words.

Many non-Christian religious or ascetic traditions—those of Zen Buddhism, Hatha yoga or Transcendental Meditation, for example—concur with the Christian ascetical insistence on the role of the body. The body's attunement to an attitude of listening or awareness, certainly of calm and silence, is a prerequisite for prayer, precisely because the mind itself needs that quietness too. Just as a fidgety body makes prayer difficult, so too does a fidgety mind. Providing we are careful to distinguish between "resting" and "sleeping," it is correct to look on the heart of prayer as resting upon the sense and conviction of the trustworthiness of the absolute.

We have already discussed earlier in this chapter the relation of liberation and salvation. The Christian who is committed to the struggle for concrete structures of human freedom will be at least implicitly aware of the fact of salvation. The response to this at the level of the whole person, as gratitude and love, can be expressed in words or in a silent resting in the conviction of *being loved and supported* by God. And the peace and sense of wholeness that arises from this naturally in its turn strengthens the conviction of salvation and consequently fires the believer for the continuing struggle for liberation. Prayer and politics, then, for the believer, are dialectically related.

If there is a close relation between prayer and politics, as we have argued, then we can ask what happens if one or other is absent or at least severely weak. If the prayer is absent, then the passionate struggle may continue, but perhaps at the price of the corruption that can grow from power. Without prayer, there is no silent trustful resting in the conviction that God is more and other than ourselves, and it is consequently too easy to move to identifying the absolute with our own efforts. This is the demonic force that can afflict the best of people and the most sacred, apparently, of institutions. On the other hand, if the politics is absent, then the trust in God is to no purpose. Without our involvement in the nexus of human social relations, what are we in the world *for*? This position, eschewing the social in the name of a private, individual religion, can produce equally evil or demonic institutions. Only the full acceptance of the political responsibility of human beings, chastened by a trust in the power which makes it all possible, produces the kind of forceful humility which characterizes truly Christian political action.

The Church and the State

Our picture of the Christian life has been a vision of human beings collaborating in building concrete structures of human freedom. Now, of course, not all those who share in this praxis of liberation constitute the Church. That term is reserved to the sub-group within the community which seeks to build the state, which seeks the praxis of liberation, out of a world-view which is Christian. In practice, they may use or choose no other methods than those adopted by their unbelieving collegues. But they will be distinguished by at least two things: their trust in the absolute as more than the sum total of human efforts, and a consequent relativization of all human, social and political strategies. There is only one rule: the permissible line of conduct is that which is inspired by and contributes to the understanding of human nature revealed in the Incarnation.

The Church can be understood, therefore, as the active Christian sub-group in civil society, working for the actualization of the state. But, and here is the problem, this defnition of the Church would be unrecognizable to very many Christians and certainly to the vast majority of Church leaders. In this respect, that of ecclesiology, as in so many other, political theology dictates a shift in our understanding. This shift is symbolized in the "basic Christian communities" of Latin America.

Too frequently, the Church is understood from first to last as an institution, to be considered alongside the state according to their different functions or "spheres of influence." The state deals with "secular" matters, for example, while the Church "takes care of souls." The Church keeps its nose out of politics, and the state does not interfere with the individual's "freedom of religion." The presumption is that there are no situations, rightly understood, where their interests can overlap, still less be in conflict. And it is just this point that we may need to question.

In the first place, the Church/state distinction is not, it seems to me, a distinction between religion and the idea of the state. The Church plays a role in religion, but it does not exhaust religious activity, and the state to which it is opposed is the concrete existing state, the more or less imperfect instantiation of the idea. To the extent, therefore, that the Church is the community of those who seek to implement concrete structures of human freedom, and to the extent to which the particular state in question is imperfect, and tending therefore towards being mere civil society, conflict between the two is unavoidable. Liberation, here, would consist precisely in the religious struggle to overcome civil society. On the other hand, the Church may be one which acquiesces in its "Sunday only" role, leaving secular concerns to the political organization, or it may be a Church which in some way becomes demonic and seeks to impose certain authoritarian principles or courses of action upon society. In these cases, the Christian community which is in some circumstances proud to call itself the

Church, may be found battling on behalf of society or humanity against the visible ecclesiastical institution.

The core of religious activity, we have discovered, is liberative praxis coupled with conscious trust in the absolute. It has an objective and a subjective dimension. The true Christian community therefore comprises those who strive to express these two dimensions of life as a community. This group may be a part of the visible, institutional Church, and is most probably a part of a political organism, although it may bestride several. As a result, it exists in tension with these two forces, that of institutional Christianity and that of civil society, each of which is claiming the subjective or objective allegiance of the individuals which comprise it. Yet the whole meaning of Christian faith as we have sought to express it here lies in the unification in the community of the subjective and objective dimensions. Faith and praxis, considered separately, lose much of their meaning. And the existence of religion is a challenge to society, putting the question about the absolute meaning of the world. But it is also a challenge to the Church.

Much earlier in this work, we described the Church as structuring the religious response of individual human beings. The Church's worship is a structured response of the individuals who make it up to the subjective conviction of a trust in the absolute which marks them out as a community. The Church provides the concrete structures within which the subjective truth-of-what-is is approached collectively. But the community which expresses itself in worship in the Church, also exists to implement concrete structures of freedom in the world. This is the way in which it builds "the kingdom," and one indispensable component of what is often referred to as "evangelization." How ironic and self-contradictory it would be, therefore, if such concrete freedoms were not actively respected within the worshipping community of the Church!

Such a vision of Church communities contains, of course, an implied critique of existing institutions. The Church has always claimed to defer to God, but today's Church has to bow, in a sense, before the sacredness of praxis. That is to say, it has to recognize the role of liberation in both expressing and creating the conditions for salvation. On the other hand, it is not simply voiceless in the face of an entirely autonomous secular activity, but watches over the preservation of the religious representations of the truth. It must toe a particularly narrow line between meddling and abdicating. It strengthens the religious vision of a humanity come of age, involved in liberative praxis. It has a voice in moral matters, insofar as it speaks against anything which interferes with responsible, autonomous human activity directed towards the implementation of concrete structures of human freedom. But it steps beyond its brief when it seeks to arbitrate between options whose respective merits should be uncovered through rational discussion.

The two great religious traditions of western Christianity have their particular weaknesses in this regard. That of Protestant ecclesiality we have frequently referred to above: it is the dualism of faith and works, kingdom and world, which leads to a deficient notion of humanity, a magical understanding of God and salvation, and a definition of the Church or community over against the world. We could add to this the excessive privatization of religion in the Protestant tradition. An emphasis on the individual conscience may lead to the kind of philanthropic liberalism for which nineteenth-century Evangelicals were justly famous, but it does not issue in a theology of human solidarity.

Catholicism's weakness is somewhat different. The incarnational perspective gives it much the right outlook for political theology, as much of what we have said must have suggested. The problem lies more in identifying the Church. The hierarchical structure of Catholicism, let us be frank, militates against concrete structures of freedom, while the theological outlook in fact encourages them. There is undoubtedly a good deal of lip-service of humanity and its authentic freedom, and there is much underlying unity of perspective between Catholic theological thinking and a political theology deriving from Hegelian incarnationalism. But the Christian anthropology which we have discerned as underpinning our political theology cannot naturally issue in authoritarianism. As Hegel rightly saw, freedom can be served by law, if it is a true natural law which protects human beings from the dictatorship of mere caprice and power-plays. But that law exists to free human nature for the actualization of the true community of the state; it is a travesty to suggest that external authority over human beings is a part of the law of their natures. Our whole incarnational anthropology exists to defend the belief that it is the internal authority of the divine-human implicit unity, and its implications, which is the true natural law. But Church authority which exists to serve the free following of natural law can too easily become a demonic destruction of that interior freedom. When that has become the case, a situation has arisen in which loyal opposition may be the order of the day. The Church is never an end in itself.

Optimism and Evil

No religious system offers a totally convincing, rational defence of its own perspective. All flounder around a little when they are confronted with the question about the existence of evil. More or less satisfactory conclusions can be reached if the religious outlook in question is prepared to say that its God is either not all-powerful, or not all-good. But if a traditional Christian position is maintained, in which God as creator is both omnipotent and all-loving, then an element of theodicy cannot be avoided. Theodicy is responsible for justifying the ways of God to human beings. At the same time, it would be safe to say that no theodicy has ever been entirely satisfactory and that the more it becomes impossible to accept the glib definition of evil as "merely negative," the more the traditional position seems under threat of collapse. In attempting to reconstruct it, however, it would be a mistake to assume that anything definitive can be said. There will be some kind of call for faith, but not a simple demand for belief in the manifestly absurd, such as "God permits evil that good may follow," or that God can see a reason we cannot for the lingering deaths of innocent children.

In the course of this work, very little has been said about suffering, beyond pointing to it as that state from which political theology seeks to remove the human race. The arguments that have been presented have necessarily been intellectual rather than emotional, and for that reason if for no other, may have seemed glib about the problems and may appear to have side-stepped or not taken account of the major concrete existential problems of our contemporary world. There is suffering and evil in alarmingly large amounts, and much of it comes from human actions. So much, you may think, for our "incarnational anthropology." There is oppression and injustice, carried out by human beings upon other, often innocent, human beings. So much for the grandiose political theology of "actualizing the state." An intellectual theology founders, does it not, when the world is shown not to operate upon or have much time for, human reason, and to be moved more by a spirit of increasingly unashamed individual and institutional greed?

In classical Christian thinking, including that of Hegel, evil is often referred to as a surd or an absence of good, as something essentially negative. And yet the presence of evil, whether personal or institutional, is an evident positive fact around us, frequently far more all-pervasive than goodness. Are Christians simply indulging in wish-fulfillment, or the kind of empty assertions in a cold world that, if not life-giving, are at least temporarily comforting?

The intention in asserting the essential negativity of evil is not, paradoxically enough, to claim that it does not exist. When evil is said to be mere "absence of good," the suggestion is that the application of good to the evil, so to speak, can be its cure. There is no attempt to say that it must be cured in this way, or that it will be, but that if honestly tried, it could be. What is the evidence for this? Is this not in its turn an assertion as empty as that of the nothingness of evil was in the first place? In attempting to outline an explanation, which is what the closing paragraphs of this book will seek to do, we shall turn again to the Hegelian world-view. The explanation is inevitably hypothetical, but it will claim to be intelligible. It will be intelligible if on the one hand it takes the world as it is with the evident existence of evil of all kinds, and, on the other, it yet provides for the existence of hope in the world. It will seek to show *that* there are grounds for hope, and *why* that hope exists. The choice *for* hope will therefore once again be the basic religious option, the choice *for* intelligibility.

We have seen at considerable length in earlier chapters that the Hegelian understanding of the relation of the world to God is that it is the "other" of the God. Since God knows, indeed, is knowledge, the concept is internal to the structure of the divine, and since God is by definition true to the divine nature, that internal or subjective concept must be expressed in an external process, by which process, in fact, the divine will come to full self-possession. Thus God posits the other of God, and in positing, creates it. The world is the other, by knowing which God comes to absolute self-possession and self-knowledge. The abstract or internal or subjective is made concrete, external, objective, on the way to being reincorporated, perfected, absolute. The reader may recall from the chapter on religion that we said there that in othering self, God is involved in a bifurcation. The other of God as Geist is nature, the other of God as infinite is finite Geist, and the true other of God is the union of nature and finite Geist, which is world.

The world, then, is not God. Nature, indeed, although created by God is other, and so alien to God. That is not to say that it is evil, but that as the other of God it is both created by and outside the control of God. If God controlled it, it would not be truly other. At the same time, God does not simply create the other, but alienates self in the other. The divine is therefore present in the world, a world which it does not control, as finite Geist. This presence is fully revealed in the Incarnation in Jesus Christ, and through this revelation the role of human beings as implicitly divine in virtue of being *finite* Geist is manifest.

We have a picture, then, of a world which is not God and which is not under God's control; but the divine is nevertheless present in the world. The manner of the divine presence, implicitly in human beings, is a real presence, and the ground of hope, but a presence as human possibility. In the person of Jesus Christ, the Incarnation reveals the true fullness of human nature, to be at one with the divine, and therefore the true potential of humanity. The possibility is limitless, therefore, but it remains possibility. It has to be actualized by individual human beings growing to their full humanity through involvement in the creation of concrete structures of human freedom. If it is possibility with which we are concerned, then that possibility might not be fulfilled.

Human beings never achieve their full potential, but what is it that holds them back? It is, in fact, human nature as a residue concept, human nature as a concept which leaves out of account the implicit union with the divine, or its secular cipher, the limitless possibility of human beings. Hegel always inveighed against those who said that the natural state was good, and organization and law were restrictions on freedom. The natural state is to be without the concrete structures of human freedom, and so the opposite of good. But there is no doubt that the condition is prevalent in the world, and that the selfishness of individuals and the institutionalized real or imagined needs of civil society are in their different ways tendencies away from corporate freedom in the idea of the state, and towards the "natural" condition. And there is equally no doubt that individual and institutional greed are the root causes of much if not most suffering in the contemporary world.

If the significance of the God-world relation for human beings is their limitless potential, then for the divine it is limited actuality. God's othering of self in the world is the free limitation of the divine within the human condition. This is one standard Christian interpretation of the Incarnation—"God emptied himself." God is therefore in the world, which world we have already said is created by God but not under the control of God, as limited to the divine potentiality within the human beings who comprise the divine objectivity. God is therefore not powerless in the world, but by the very nature of the world limited to the expression of the divine power through the possibilities and the limitations of human beings. It is this, when all is said and done, that makes human activity divine agency, and the implementation of concrete structures of human freedom identical with the building of the kingdom, even when it is not aware of that identity.

If the world is the other of God, then, and the only alternative is that it should be God himself, and so not world at all, its independence must give it its own pace and logic which is by definition out of divine control. The possibility of reconciliation or redemption is a gift, however, the gift of God's presence in the world as finite Geist, preferring liberation in the shape of human potentiality. The full exercise of that potentiality may be impossible, but it is interesting to note that it would result in the full return to the divine, the completion of the cycle.

Our theological vision, then, might be better described as comic than optimistic. It does not argue that all is or will be well in the best of all possible worlds, and it can quite accept, at least in theory, that the human rejection of its potentiality could result in a nuclear war. But it does claim that the solution to our failings is within our grasp, because the God-given goodness and reason of our human natures is always there, implicit and potential if not actualized. That is to say, the triumph of good over evil is speculatively accomplished. God is both far away and near. The stage of history is the other of God, and so God is distant, and the responsibility is ours. But God is at the heart of human possibility as it seeks to build a community of freedom. To say therefore that the speculative resolution has been achieved is not to deny that the political theology plods on. Salvation/liberation is already but not yet. The fullness of the eschaton has to be worked for and to be awaited. To say that God has brought about salvation in the divine presence in human potentiality, is simply the obverse of saying that in its existential transformation into structures of human liberation, it is up to us.

Notes

Introduction

1. The primary text for the interrelations of ideology and liberation theology is undoubtedly Juan Luis Segundo, *The Liberation of Theology* (London: Gill and Macmillan, 1977).

2. Recent political theology, especially the work of J. B. Metz, recognizes that it has much to learn from liberation theology emerging from the so-called third world. See especially Metz, *The Emergent Church: The Future of Christianity in a Post-Bourgeois World* (London: SCM, 1981).

3. *Political Theology* (Philadelphia: Fortress Press, 1974), p. 59.

4. See Segundo, *The Liberation of Theology*, chapter 3 and Gustavo Gutierrez, *A Theology of Liberation* (Maryknoll, New York: Orbis Books, 1973), which latter book is of course *the* classic in the literature of liberation theology.

5. See, for example, J. B. Metz, *Theology of the World* (New York: 1969), or the same author's *Faith In History and Society: Toward a Practical Fundamental Theology* (New York: Seabury Press, 1980), especially chapter 3. Chapters 5–8 of Soelle's *Political Theology* constitute the best introduction to her opinions. For a recent sympathetic but trenchant critique of German contemporary political theology see John B. Cobb, Jr., *Process Theology as Political Theology* (Philadelphia, PA: The Westminster Press, 1982).

6. *Communication and the Evolution of Society* (Boston: Beacon Press, 1976), p. 95.

7. On this see especially Hegel's introductory lecture in *Vorlesungen über die Philosophie der Geschichte*. This work is volume eleven of the *Sämtliche Werke, Jubiläumsausgabe in zwanzig Bänder*, edited by Hermann Glockner (Stuttgart: Fr. Frommanns Verlag, 1958). A somewhat unsatisfactory English translation is available in *The Philosophy of History* (New York: Dover Publications, 1956). In all subsequent references to Hegel's text, I shall refer in abbreviated form to VPG and LPH respectively, adding the volume and page number for the *Sämtliche Werke*, abbreviated to SW. In all citations of other of Hegel's works, I shall follow the same practice of citing both German and English texts, and adding the reference to SW where appropriate. I have selected the *Sämtliche Werke*, the so-called *Jubiläumsausgabe*, simply because it remains the most readily-available German text.

Chapter I

1. A full list of these studies appears in the bibliography, but I am most deeply indebted to the following: Franz Rosenzweig, *Hegel und der Staat* (Munich and Berlin: R. Oldenbourg, 1920); Shlomo Avineri, *Hegel's Theory of the Modern State* (London: Cambridge University Press, 1972); George Armstrong Kelly, *Hegel's Retreat from Eleusis: Studies in Political Thought* (Princeton: Princeton University Press, 1978); and Charles Taylor, *Hegel and Modern Society* (Cambridge: Cambridge University Press, 1979).

2. Rosenzweig, 1:42–46, 87–98, 101–219; Avineri, pp. 1–114; and see also George Armstrong Kelly, *Idealism, Politics and History: Sources of Hegelian Thought* (Cambridge: Cambridge University Press, 1969), passim.

3. Herman Nohl, ed., *Hegels theologische Jugendschriften* (Tübingen: J.C.B. Mohr, 1907), pp. 345–351. An English translation is available in *Early Theological Writings*, translated by T. M. Knox, with an introduction and fragments translated by Richard Kroner (Philadelphia: University of Pennsylvania Press, 1971), pp. 309–319.

4. The texts of Hegel's Jena period have been among the first volumes to appear in the new standard edition of his works: *Gesammelte Werke, in Verbindung mit der deutschen Forschungsgemeinschaft, herausgegeben von der rheinisch-westfälischen Akademie der Wissenschaften.* (Hamburg: Felix Meiner Verlag, 1968 –).

5. *Enzyklopädie der philosophischen Wissenschaften im Grundrisse* (1830). The most up-to-date edition of this work is that edited by Friedhelm Nicolin and Otto Poggeler (Hamburg: Felix Meiner Verlag, 7th edition, 1969), but since this does not include the Zusätze, I shall normally refer to the relevant volume of the *Jubiläumsausgabe.* English translations of the three parts of the Encyclopaedia are available: *Hegel's Logic, Being Part One of the Encyclopaedia of the Philosophical Sciences* (1830), translated by William Wallace, with a foreword by J. N. Findlay (Oxford: Clarendon Press, 1975); *Hegel's Philosophy of Nature*, translated by A. V. Miller, with a foreword by J. N. Findlay (Oxford: Clarendon Press, 1970); *Hegel's Philosophy of Mind, Being Part Three of the Encyclopaedia of the Philosophical Sciences* (1830), translated by William Wallace, together with the *Zusätze* in Boumann's text (1845), translated by A. V. Miller, with a foreword by J. N. Findlay (Oxford: Clarendon Press, 1971). Subsequent references will be to Enc., giving first the numbered section, then the page number to the *Jubiläumsausgabe*, finally the page number to the English text, although in fact the translations are my own.

6. *Grundlinien der Philosophie des Rechts*, edited by Johannes Hoffmeister (Hamburg: Felix Meiner Verlag, 1955). The English version is *Hegel's Philosophy of Right*, translated with notes by T. M. Knox (London: Oxford University Press, 1967). Subsequent references will be to PR, giving first the numbered section, then page references first to Hoffmeister and secondly to Knox, whose English translation I am using except where otherwise noted.

7. See Enc., Zusatz to §258, and §549.

8. In translating Hegel, one of the major problems is the central word, *Geist*. The two obvious possibilities are "mind" and "spirit," and translators vary as to their preference. Unfortunately, in English "mind" suggests the purely earthbound intellect, and "spirit" is too ethereal to do full justice to the German original. With some misgivings, I have decided for the purposes of this work to retain the word *Geist*, although at some points I have been forced to settle for "finite spirits" rather than "finite Geists," and I have felt that *geistlich* had to be translated, inevitably as "spiritual," if the use of loan-words was not to get entirely out of hand.

9. *Wissenschaft der Logik* (volumes 4–5 in SW). There is an English version, *Hegel's Science of Logic*, translated by A. V. Miller, with a foreword by J. N. Findlay (London: George Allen and Unwin, 1969).

10. See Introduction, n. 5.

11. *Vorlesungen über die Philosophie der Religion*, edited by Georg Lasson, four volumes in two (Hamburg: Felix Meiner Verlag, 1925–30). The text is also available in the *Jubiläumsausgabe*, volumes XV–XVI. The full English translation, following the text of SW, is *Lectures on Philosophy of Religion*, translated by E. B. Speirs and J. B. Sanderson, three volumes (New York: Humanities Press, 1962). A new English critical edition of the third part of the lectures, following more closely the Lasson edition, although varying frequently from it, is *The Christian Religion*, edited and translated by Peter C. Hodgson, AAR Texts and Translations Series, no. 2 (Missoula, MT: Scholars Press, 1979).

12. Enc. §§483–552.

13. Enc. §377; SW X,9; PM 1.

14. Enc. §§245–376.

15. Enc. §377; SW X,9; PM 1.

16. Enc., *Zusatz* to §377; SW X,10; PM 1.

17. Enc., *Zusatz* to §381; SW X,20.

18. Two well-known and justly respected authorities who adopt such a line are Charles Taylor and Emil Fackenheim. See Taylor's *Modern Society*, pp. 66–68 and his *Hegel* (Cambridge: Cambridge University Press, 1975), pp. 537–571; and Fackenheim's *The Religious Dimension in Hegel's Thought* (Bloomington, Ind.: Indiana University Press, 1967), especially the final chapter.

19. The question of the relation of religion and philosophy in Hegel's thinking is, of course, the rock on which early Hegelianism foundered, and the "right" and "left" wing variants broke apart. A most outstanding recent work to discuss this in great detail is *Hegelianism*, by John Edward Toews (Cambridge: Cambridge University Press, 1980). Toews is especially valuable for charting the presence of these different understandings of Hegel long before Hegel's death, in the writings of minor and sometimes long-forgotten disciples of the master. In contemporary Hegelian study, the foremost descendent of "right wing" Hegelianism, at least in the sense that he defends a thoroughly Christian interpretation of Hegel, has to be Quentin

Lauer. This is clearest in his most recent book, which unfortunately appeared too late for all but the most niggardly notice in this work, *Hegel's Concept of God* (Albany: SUNY Press, 1982). Finally, Hegel's own words should not be lightly dismissed (see, for example, the lengthy Zusatz to Enc. §381).

20. Lauer, *Hegel's Concept of God*, p. 138. The work with which Lauer is in sympathetic dialogue here is Michael Theunissen's *Hegels Lehre vom absoluten Geist als theologisch-politischer Traktat* (Berlin: Walter de Gruyter, 1970). Both Lauer and Theunissen, it should be noted, do not commit themselves at this point on the general question of whether Hegel's Geist is dependent on the world, but restrict themselves to what Hegel is attempting to show in Enc. §564.

21. Enc., *Zusatz* to §381; SW X,21; PM 9.

22. Enc., *Zusatz* to §381; SW X,24; PM 11.

23. VPG; SW XI,37; LPH 11.

24. Enc., *Zusatz* to §385; SW X,42; PM 21.

25. Enc., *Zusatz* to §386; SW X,43; PM 23.

26. Enc., *Zusatz* to §386; SW X,44–45; PM 24.

27. Enc., §518; SW X,399; PM 255.

28. PR, Preface; Hoff. 3; Knox 1.

29. Enc. §483.

30. Enc. §484.

31. PR §4; Hoff. 28; Knox 20.

32. On this see the comments of Knox in the translator's foreword to *The Philosophy of Right*, p. vi.

33. Enc. §502.

34. Enc. §485; SW X,382–3; PM 485.

35. Enc. §488–492; SW X,385–6; PM 244–5. PR 41–71; Hoff. 55–79; Knox 40–57.

36. Enc. §488; SW X,386; PM 244.

37. Enc. §490.

38. Enc. §501–2.

39. Enc. §503; SW X,392; PM 249.

40. Addn. to PR 106, Knox p. 248. Hoffmeister does not print the additional material which was added to Hegel's original by Eduard Gans in vol. viii of Hegel's *Werke*, published in Berlin in 1833, with second and third editions in 1840 and 1854. Gans brought in material from lecture notes, and in Knox's translation this has been removed from the main body of the text and collected in an appendix. Where we quote from this material, it will be referred to as Addition (Addn.), to distinguish it from Hegel's own *Zusätze*, which of course remain in Hoffmeister's edition. And on these occasions we shall give a reference to Gans (2nd edition) rather than to Hoffmeister. The rationale for removing Gans' insertions can be read in Hoffmeister's preface to PR (see note 5 above), pp. vii–xvii. This Addn. is in Gans. p. 145.

41. Zusatz to PR §106; Hoff. 101–2; Knox 75.
42. Enc. §513; SW X,397; PM 253–254.
43. Enc. §514; SW X,397; PM 254.
44. PR §145; Hoff. 143; Knox 105.
45. PR §146; Hoff. 143; Knox 106.
46. PR §147; Hoff. 143; Knox 106.
47. PR §151; Hoff. 147; Knox 108–9.
48. PR §156; Hoff. 147; Knox 110.
49. PR §158; Hoff. 149; Knox 110.
50. PR §159; Hoff. 149–50; Knox 111.
51. See Enc. §522 and PR 177, 181.
52. PR §181; Hoff, 164; Knox 122.
53. Ibid.
54. Addn. to PR §181; Gans 240; Knox 266.
55. PR §181; Hoff. 165; Knox 122.
56. PR §183; Hoff. 165; Knox 123.
57. PR §184; Hoff. 165; Knox 123.
58. Zusatz to PR §189; Hoff. 170; Knox 126–7.
59. PR §190; Hoff. 171; Knox 127.
60. Zusatz to PR §194; Hoff. 172; Knox 128.
61. See PR §195.
62. PR §196; Hoff. 173; Knox 128–9.
63. PR §199; Hoff. 174; Knox 129. It is, of course, quite certain that Hegel saw a negative side to the role of labour in the society of his times. This is first evident in the treatment of labour in the *System der Sittlichkeit* and in the *Jenaer Realphilosophie*, but at this stage of the PR, Hegel is simply not concerned to be critical. In the *System*, edited by George Lasson (Hamburg: F. Meiner Verlag, 2nd edition, 1923), see pp. 433–435. ET: *Hegel's System of Ethical Life and First Philosophy of Spirit*, edited and translated by H. S. Harris and T. M. Knox (Albany: State University of New York Press, 1979). The *Realphilosophie* is available in *Jenaer Realphilosophie*, edited by J. Hoffmeister (Hamburg: F. Meiner, 1967), which is a reprint of the original edition, entitled *Jenaer Realphilosophie II: Die Vorlesungen von* 1805/6. See p. 218. There is no English translation of this volume.
   The most useful discussion of Hegel's view of labour in this earlier period is in Avineri, pp. 87–98.
64. PR §200; Hoff. 175; Knox 130.
65. On this, see Emil Fackenheim, "On the Actuality of the Rational and the Rationality of the Actual," *Review of Metaphysics*, 23 (1970): 690–8.
66. *Hegel*, p. 437.
67. For Avineri, this self-destructiveness is what grounds the necessity of the state; see *Modern State*, p. 99.
68. PR §201; Hoff. 175; Knox 131.
69. Avineri, *Modern State*, p. 104.

70. PR §203; Hoff. 176; Knox 131.
71. PR §204; Hoff. 177; Knox 132.
72. PR §205; Hoff. 177; Knox 132.
73. PR §206; Hoff. 178; Knox 132.
74. PR §207; Hoff. 179; Knox 133.
75. See Enc. §380.
76. PR §239.
77. PR §195.
78. PR §241; Hoff. 190; Knox 148–9.
79. PR §243; Hoff. 191; Knox 149–50.
80. Addn. to PR §244; Gans 296; Knox 277.
81. PR §245; Hoff. 201; Knox 150.
82. PR §255; Hoff. 206; Knox 154.
83. Nos. 91 & 92, pp. 361–2.
84. PR §252; Hoff. 204; Knox 153.
85. PR §256; Hoff. 207; Knox 155.
86. Ibid.

Chapter II

1. See Avineri, *Modern State*, pp. 116–7.
2. See, for example, PR, the *Zusatz* to §258.
3. The German text of this work, *The German Constitution*, is included in GW, 4, *Jenaer kritische Schriften*. For the ET, see *Hegel's Political Writings*, translated by T. M. Knox, with an introductory essay by Z. A. Pelczynski (Oxford: Clarendon Press, 1964), pp. 141–242. The introductory essay attempts to defend the unusual thesis that Hegel's political writings can be appreciated without any recourse to his more strictly philosophical writings, a thesis which, correct or not, Hegel would have viewed with horror. For a discussion of this essay, see Avineri's excellent chapter three in *Modern State*, pp. 34–61.
4. PR §273; Hoff. 235; Knox 176.
5. The word *Stände* can be translated either as "classes," or as "estates." Hegel feels that the use of the same word for both the social and the political reality supports his case.
6. PR, *Zusatz* to §303; Hoff. 265; Knox 198.
7. PR §305; Hoff, 266; Knox 199.
8. PR §307.
9. PR, *Zusatz* to §308.
10. See PR §312–315, and §316 following.
11. Preface to PR; Hoff. 16; Knox 11.
12. PR §273; Hoff. 235; Knox 176.
13. Hoff. 214–5; Knox 160–1.

14. *Zusatz* to Enc. §379; SW X,17; PM 6.

15. SW X,31; PM 15.

16. Lauer, pp. 141–143.

17. Fackenheim, *The Religious Dimension*, pp. 75–112.

18. PR §258; Hoff. 208; Knox 155–6.

19. *Christologies and Cultures: Toward a Typology of Religious World-views* (The Hague: Mouton, 1974), pp. 151–5.

20. Ibid., p. 150.

21. On this, see Gunther Rohrmoser's interesting discussion of the Marxist critique of Hegel's view of the state, in "Die theologischen Voraussetzungen der hegelschen Lehre vom Staat," *Hegel-Studien, Beiheft* 1, *Heidelberger Hegel-Tage*, 1962 (Bonn: Bouvier, 1964), herausgegeben von Hans-Georg Gadamer, pp. 239–46.

22. *Individuum und Gemeinschaft bei Hegel: Band I, Hegel im Spiegel der Interpretationen* (Berlin & New York: Walter de Gruyter, 1977), pp. 43–58, especially pp. 44–5.

23. Barth, *Protestant Theology in the Nineteenth Century: Its Background and History* (London: SCM, 1972), p. 535.

24. Ibid., p. 536.

25. Feuerbach, "Vorläufige Thesen zur Reformation der Philosophie," in *Kleinere Schriften II: 1839–46* (Berlin: Akademie-Verlag, 1970), edited by Werner Schuffenhauer and Wolfgang Harich, pp. 261–2. See also Ottman, *Individuum*, p. 44.

26. On the question of the historical nature of metaphysical truth, see Emil Fackenheim, *Metaphysics and Historicity* (Milwaukee: Marquette University Press, 1961).

27. *Kleinere Schriften II*, p. 258.

28. "The German Ideology," in *Writings of the Young Marx on Philosophy and Society* (Garden City, NY: Doubleday Anchor, 1967), p. 407.

29. See the sixth of Marx's "Theses on Feuerbach," in *Karl Marx: the Essential Writings* (New York: Harper & Row, 1972), edited by Frederic L. Bender, p. 154.

30. Marx, *Essential Writings*, p. 130.

31. On this, see Karl Marx, *Critique of Hegel's "Philosophy of Right"* (Cambridge: CUP, 1970), edited by Joseph O'Malley, pp. xxix–xxx.

32. Edited by Johannes Hoffmeister (Hamburg: Felix Meiner, 1952). ET: *The Phenomenology of Mind*, translated with an introduction and notes by J. B. Baillie (New York: Harper & Row, 1967).

33. Marx, *Essential Writings*, p. 134.

34. Ibid., p. 137.

35. Karl Marx and Friedrich Engels, *Basic Writings on Politics and Philosophy* (Garden City, NY: Anchor Books, 1959), pp. 262–3.

36. Marx, *Essential Writings*, p. 141.

37. Marx, *Critique of Hegel's "Philosophy of Right,"* p. 91.

38. Ibid., p. 11.

39. Ibid., p. 9.

40. Michael Theunissen presents a very useful discussion of later Marxist interpretation of Hegel in his *Hegels Lehre vom absoluten Geist als theologisch-politischer Traktat* (Berlin: Walter de Gruyter, 1970), pp. 3–59. Theunissen discusses the views of Lukacs, Garaudy, Ritter and Habermas on Hegel's political views, and Adorno's critique of the theology. He thinks that they ignore Hegel's claim that the revolutionary principle is the death and resurrection of Christ, seeing revolutionary subjectivity as having been sold out in favor of the *Weltgeist*. The really central issue, says Theunissen, is the relation between the Absolute and objective totality, and the Marxists want to collapse the former into the latter. The author seeks his evidence for the Absolute's transcendence of objective totality, and thus the grounding of human freedom, in Hegel's *Glauben und Wissen* (GW, Band 4).

41. PR §257; Hoff. 207; Knox 155.

42. PR §260; Hoff. 214–5; Knox 160.

43. Hoff; 208; Knox 156–7.

44. Enc. §537; SW X,410; PM 264.

45. Enc. *Zusatz* to §382; SW X,31; PM 15.

46. Ibid.

47. See Rosenzweig, 2:169–173. Rosenszweig characterizes the individual of abstract right as one of a mere multitude which is not yet a community. The individual will "hat nur dadurch Anspruch auf Verwirklichung, dass er dem Willen aller anderen den gleichen Anspruch zuerkennt." In the area of morality, this is reversed, and all the individual knows is the moral will understood as the categorical imperative, "den Willen einer idealen Gemeinschaft, und diese nicht neben seinem eigenen Willen, sondern als einerlei mit ihm." But the sphere of the ethical life brings the two together, and the individual recognizes the community as external to self, and so that there is a reciprocity between individual and community. The relation of state and individual is seen by Rosenszweig as necessary because it is inescapable: "Er darf zwischen dem 'Zufall' seiner besonderen Stellung und der Notwendigkeit einem Staate überhaupt anzugehören, nicht scheiden."

48. PR, *Zusatz* to §258; Hoff. 208; Knox 156.

49. Ibid.

50. PR §133; Hoff. 119; Knox 90.

51. PR, *Zusatz* to §135; Hoff. 120; Knox 90.

52. See the discussion in Taylor, *Hegel*, pp. 370 following.

53. Taylor, *Hegel*, p. 373.

54. Ibid., p. 374.

55. Ibid., p. 376.

56. Ibid., p. 386.

57. Ibid., p. 387.

58. Ibid., pp. 208–11.
59. Ibid., p. 539.
60. PR §322; Hoff. 278; Knox 208.
61. PR §332–4 and 339.
62. PR §340; Hoff. 288; Knox 216.
63. See Introduction, note 6.
64. PR §342; Hoff. 289; Knox 216.
65. PR §344; Hoff. 290; Knox 217.
66. VPG, SW XI,34; LPH 12.
67. VPG, SW XI,15; LPH 8.
68. VPG, SW XI,41–42; LPH 15.
69. VPG, SW XI,45; LPH 17.
70. VPG, SW XI,52; LPH 23.
71. VPG, SW XI,70; LPH 38.
72. VPG, SW XI,71; LPH 39.
73. See Kenley R. Dove, "Hegel's Phenomenological Method," *Review of Metaphysics* 23 (1970): pp. 615–641.

Chapter III

1. See the final bibliography under: Asveld, Brito, Bruaire, Chapelle, Crites, Fackenheim, Koch, Küng, Lauer, Marsch, Muller, Reardon, Rohrmoser, Schmidt, Theunissen and Yerkes.
2. Chapelle, Marsch, Muller.
3. Bruaire, Fackenheim, Koch, Theunissen.
4. Brito, Küng, Yerkes.
5. Asveld, Rohrmoser.
6. Albert Chapelle, *Hegel et la Religion* (Paris: Editions universitaires, 3 vols., 1967), volume 3, "Annexes," pp. 94–97.
7. *Phän.* SW II,517; Baillie 685.
8. Ibid. SW II,519; Baillie 687.
9. Enc. §564; SW X,453–4; PM 298.
10. Enc. §554; SW X,446; PM 292.
11. *Hegels Lehre*, p. 118.
12. *Ibid., pp.* 103–4, 118.
13. See note 10.
14. See Enc. §554; SW X,446; PM 292.
15. Enc. §555; SW X,447; PM 292–3.
16. Ibid.
17. Ibid.
18. Enc. §565; SW X,454; PM 299.
19. Enc. §564; SW X,453; PM 297.
20. Enc. §573; SW X,458; PM 302.

21. The only translation of the entirety of the VPR is the Speirs and Sanderson edition, which follows the text of the *Werke*, but is more than a little idiosyncratic in places in its English rendering. Nevertheless, the text is easier to follow than the Lasson text, at least for the first two parts. I have therefore quoted from the *Werke* in my own translation wherever I have needed references to the first two parts of the lectures, and for the third part I have referenced Lasson, and Hodgson's English critical edition (*The Christian Religion*, edited and translated by Peter C. Hodgson. AAR Texts and Translations Series, no. 2. Missoula, MT: Scholars Press, 1979), using Hodgson's translation. It is good to know that Hodgson and Walter Jaeschke of the Hegel-Archiv in Bochum are collaborating on furthering a definitive edition of the entire lectures, in both German and English languages.

22. VPR; SW XV,78; LPR I, 61.

23. VPR; SW XV,78; LPR I, 62.

24. VPR; SW XV,80–81; LPR I, 64.

25. VPR; SW XV,83; LPR I, 69.

26. Ibid.

27. VPR; SW XV,86; LPR I, 70.

28. Such absence of relation would characterize the religion of pure fear, and might extend to those forms of Christianity which emphasize the "absolute qualitative distinction" between finite and infinite. Such a distinction would, for Hegel, be a case of a "bad" infinite.

29. Enc. §574; SW X,453; PM 298.

30. VPR; SW XV,99; LPR I, 83-4.

31. VPR; Lasson IV, 6; Hodgson 10.

32. The schematic presentation on pp. 326–7 seems to me more complex than necessary: the point at issue in the relation of economic and immanent trinity is simply that if God is essentially self-manifestation, then what is manifest in the finite is a revelation of what is true in Geist in itself. We have already come to understand the internal structure of the concept as identical to the form of the relations between concept, nature and Geist, and we can look at God's "internal nature" so to speak, as standing in the same relation to God's revelation—otherwise it would be, not revelation, but obscurity.

33. Hodgson, pp. 169–229; cf. Lasson IV, 130–174.

34. There are obvious parallels here between the christology of Hegel as we have so far uncovered it, and that of a transcendental Thomist like Rahner. Both are concerned with a form of circularity between implicit anthropological structures, human being as "graced nature" or as finite spirits, and the revelation of the truth of these structures through the event of Christ, who makes these implicit structures explicit in his person. The parallel could be extended to the identification of christology with soteriology. It is the revelation of who Jesus Christ is, a human at one with the divine, which uncovers the reconciliatory move. For Hegel this occurs in

the incarnate's death and resurrection. For Rahner, I suspect, the death and resurrection are the events which designate this man as the Christ, *ordo cognoscendi*. See for example Rahner's *Foundations of Christian Faith: An Introduction to the Idea of Christianity* (New York: The Seabury Press, 1978), especially pp. 208–212.

35. VPR; Hodgson 171; Lasson 131.
36. VPR; Hodgson 176; Lasson 136.
37. VPR; Hodgson 181; Lasson 141.
38. VPR; Hodgson 177; Lasson 137.
39. VPR; Hodgson 186–190; Lasson, 142–155.
40. VPR; Hodgson 190; Lasson, 148.
41. For a modern christology influenced clearly by Hegel, see Dorothee Soelle, *Christ the Representative* (Philadelphia: Fortress Press, 1967), esp. pp. 140–142.
42. Hodgson 201; Lasson IV, 157.
43. Ibid.
44. VPR; Hodgson 202; Lasson IV, 158.
45. VPR; Hodgson 203–4; Lasson IV, 159–160.
46. VPR; Hodgson 212; Lasson IV, 167.
47. VPR; Hodgson 214; Lasson IV, 168.
48. VPR Hodgson 268–276; Lasson IV, 108–215.
49. Enc. §552; SW X, 433–445; PM 282–291. PR §270; Hoff. 220–233; Knox 164–174. VPR; SW XV, 256–267; LPR I, 246–257. VPG; SW XI, 82–87; LPH 48–52.
50. Enc. §552; SW X,434; PM 282.
51. Enc. §552; SW X,435; PM 283.
52. Enc. §552; SW X,439; PM 287.
53. PR §270; Hoff 222; Knox 166.
54. PR §270; Hoff 221; Knox 165.
55. PR §270; Hoff 223; Knox 167.
56. PR §270; Hoff 229; Knox 171.
57. PR §270; Hoff 230; Knox 172.
58. VPR; SW XV,256–267; LPR I,246–57.
59. VPG; SW XI,84; LPH 50.
60. See, for example, the discussion between Quentin Lauer, James Doull and Charles D. Darrett in *Hegel and the Philosophy of Religion: The Wofford Symposium* (The Hague: Martinus Nijhoff, 1970), edited by Darrel E. Christensen, pp. 261–295.
61. VPR; Hodgson 295–7; Lasson IV, 231–2.
62. VPR; Hodgson 296; Lasson IV,228.
63. VPR; Hodgson 296; Lasson IV,228.
64. VPR; Hodgson 297; Lasson IV,228.
65. VPR; Hodgson 296; Lasson IV,228.

66. In his *The Invisible Religion* (New York: The Macmillan Company, 1967). Hereafter: *IR*.
67. *IR*, p. 12.
68. *IR*, p. 23.
69. *IR*, p. 26.
70. *IR*, p. 27.
71. *IR*, p. 37.
72. *IR*, p. 38.
73. *IR*, p. 43.
74. *IR*, p. 44.
75. *IR*, p. 45.
76. *IR*, p. 46.
77. *IR*, p. 70.
78. *IR*, p. 79.
79. *IR*, p. 101.
80. See for example VPR; SW XV, 65–75; LPR I, 48–58.
81. See Enc., §488.

Chapter IV

1. David Martin, *The Religious and the Secular: Studies in Secularisation* (New York: Schocken Books, 1969). Peter L. Berger, *The Sacred Canopy: Elements of a Sociological Theory of Religion* (Doubleday & Co.: New York, 1967). Walter Jaeschke, *Die Suche nach den eschatologischen Wurzeln der Geschichtsphilosophie: Eine historische Kritik der Säkularisierungsthese* (Munchen: Chr. Kaiser Verlag, 1976). Eberhard Jungel, "Säkularisierung—theologische Anmerkungen zum Begriff einer weltlichen Welt," in *Christliche Freiheit im Dienst am Menschen*, edited by Karl Herbert (Frankfurt-am-Main: Verlag Otto Lembeck, 1972), pp. 163–8. Friedrich Gogarten, *Verhängnis und Hoffnung der Neuzeit: Die Säkularisierung als theologisches Problem* (München: Siebenstern Taschenbuch Verlag, 1958); ET. *Despair and Hope in Our Time* (Philadelphia and Boston: Pilgrim Press, 1970). Thomas Luckmann, *The Invisible Religion: The Problem of Religion in Modern Society* (New York: Macmillan, 1967). Edward Schillebeeckx, *God: The Future of Man* (New York, Sheed and Ward, 1968).
2. *The Invisible Religion*, especially pp. 17–27.
3. See David Martin, "Towards Eliminating the Concept of Secularization," in *Penguin Survey of Sociology of Religion* (Baltimore: Penguin Books, 1965).
4. There are a multitude of possible examples of this outlook, beginning from Kierkegaard and Barth. Later in this chapter I shall make most use of Friedrich Gogarten's *Despair and Hope in Our Time*.

5. *God: The Future of Man*, p. 67.
6. Ibid., p. 56.
7. Ibid., pp. 57–8.
8. Ibid., pp. 170–5.
9. *The Invisible Religion*, pp. 107–114.
10. *Penguin Survey*, pp. 16–17.
11. J. A. T. Robinson, *Honest To God* (Philadelphia: Westminster Press, 1963), and David L. Edwards, *The "Honest to God" Debate: Some Reactions to the Book, "Honest to God"* (Philadelphia: Westminster Press, 1963).
12. *The Myth of God Incarnate*, edited by John Hick (Philadelphia: Westminster Press, 1977). This book was countered by many conservative arguments, in particular by *The Truth of God Incarnate*, edited by Michael Green (Grand Rapids: Eerdmans, 1977). For a recent re-appraisal of the whole discussion, and of the history of recent Anglican christology, see Brian Hebblethwaite, "The Propriety of the Doctrine of the Incarnation as a Way of Interpreting Christ," *Scottish Journal of Theology* 33 (1980): 201–222.
13. "Heidegger and Theology," *Review of Metaphysics* 18 (1964): 207–233.
14. Ibid., p. 226.
15. Ibid., p. 219.
16. See Lakeland, "Hegel's Atheism," *The Heythrop Journal* 21 (1980): 245–259.
17. *Meaning in History* (Chicago: University of Chicago Press, 1949), p. 59.
18. "Hegels Aufhebung der christlichen Religion," in *Einsichten: Gerhard Kruger zum 60. Geburtstag*, edited by Klaus Gehler and Richard Schaeffler (Frankfurt-am-Main: Vittorio Klostermann, 1962), pp. 156–203. There is an interesting response to Löwith's argument by Carl G. Schweitzer, "Zur Methode der Hegel-Interpretation: Eine Entgegnung auf Karl Löwiths 'Hegels Aufhebung der christlichen Religion'," *Neue Zeitschrift fur Systematische Theologie und Religionsphilosophie* 5 (1963): 248–262.
19. *Protestant Theology in the Nineteenth Century* (London: SCM Press, 1972), pp. 384–421.
20. VPR, Lasson I, 49.
21. Barth, p. 417.
22. Barth, p. 418.
23. Barth, p. 419.
24. Barth, p. 420.
25. Emil Fackenheim would be a good example of someone who from an obviously non-incarnational standpoint. finds the God-hypothesis of secularization myth problematic. See his *God's Presence in History: Jewish Affirmations and Philosophical Reflections* (New York: New York University Press, 1970), pp. 35–66.

26. In *Theology of Culture* (Oxford: University Press, 1975), pp. 10–29.

27. Tillich, p. 25.

28. Tillich, p. 11.

29. Tillich, p. 13.

30. Tillich, p. 10.

31. Tillich, p. 21.

32. Lauer, *The Wofford Symposium*, p. 275.

33. Tillich, p. 14.

34. Tillich, p. 15.

35. Tillich, p. 15–16.

36. Tillich, p. 18.

37. For a thorough study of Gogarten's positions, see Larry Shiner, *The Secularization of History: an Introduction to the Theology of F. Gogarten* (Nashville and New York: The Abingdon Press, 1966).

38. Gogarten, p. 68.

39. Gogarten, p. 66.

40. Gogarten, p. 150.

41. Gogarten, pp. 132, 135.

42. Gogarten, p. 152.

43. Gogarten, pp. 161–2.

44. Ernst Troeltsch, "An Apple from the Tree of Kierkegaard," in *The Beginnings of Dialectic Theology*, edited by James M. Robinson (Richmond, Virginia: John Knox Press, 1968), pp. 311–16.

45. *Beginnings*, p. 312.

46. Ibid., p. 312–3.

47. Ibid., p. 314–5.

48. Ibid., p. 315.

49. Shiner, *The Secularization of History*, and "Toward a Theology of Secularization," *Journal of Religion*, 45 (1965): 279–295.

50. *The Secularization of History*, pp. 99–101.

51. Ibid., p. 103.

52. Ibid., p. 107.

53. In *Ecclesial Man* (Philadelphia: Fortress Press, 1976), and especially in *Ecclesial Reflection: An Anatomy of Theological Method* (Philadelphia: Fortress Press, 1982), pp. 3–168.

54. James Yerkes' *The Christology of Hegel* is undoubtedly the best single work on the subject.

55. This idea is common throughout Rahner's works. See especially "Nature and Grace," *Theological Investigations IV* (Baltimore: Helicon, 1966), pp. 165–188.

56. Such a view is quite apparent in the ecclesiology of Juan Luis Segundo. See *A Theology for Artisans of a New Humanity, Volume One: The Community Called Church* (Maryknoll, New York: Orbis, 1973).

Chapter V

1. From an unpublished lecture, quoted in Lakeland, "Responding to Liberation Theology," *The Month* 241 (January 1980): 12-15.
2. See Segundo, *The Liberation of Theology*, passim.
3. Ibid., p. 8.
4. See especially Jon Sobrino, *Christology at the Crossroads: A Latin American Approach* (London: SCM, 1978).
5. Soelle, *Political Theology*, pp. 59-64.
6. For the full discussion, refer to the second major section of chapter II, "The Ethical Substance."
7. PR, Zusatz to §258; Hoff. 208; Knox 156.
8. Ibid.
9. Jose Miranda, *Marx and the Bible* (New York: Orbis, 1975), p. 213.
10. Rubem Alves, *A Theology of Human Hope* (St. Meinrad, Indiana: Abbey Press, 1975), p. 95.
11. Sobrino, *Crossroads*, pp. 362-370.
12. In support of this, Miranda quotes Gerhard Friedrich from TDNT 2:726, writing on *euangelion*: "A new message is not expected with the dawn of God's kingdom. What will be proclaimed has been known from the time of deutero-Isaiah. The longing is that it should be proclaimed. Hence in contemporary literature, the messenger and the act of proclamation are much more important than the message. The new feature is not the message but the eschatological act." (Miranda, *Marx*, p. 213).
13. Miranda, *Marx*, p. 172.
14. Miranda, *Marx*, pp. 172-3.
15. Sobrino, *Crossroads*, p. 356.
16. Sobrino, *Crossroads*, p. 357.
17. Preface to PR, Knox p. 12.
18. The need, of course, is to find a middle position which admits of a form of presence as more than a future promise.
19. Alves, *Human Hope*, p. 97.
20. Ibid., p. 94.
21. Louis Althusser and Etienne Balibar, *Reading Capital* (London: NLB, 1977), p. 93.
22. Ibid., p. 94.
23. Ibid., p. 95.
24. PR §333; Hoff. 285; Knox 214.
25. Ibid.
26. Such an assumption lies behind, for example, *North-South: A Programme for Survival* (London: Pan, 1980), the report of the independent commission on international development issues, chaired by former West German chancellor, Willy Brandt.
27. See, for example, PR §324-328 and Enc. §546.

28. PR §340.

29. Basic Christian Communities (*communidades eclesiales de base*) arose out of the particular circumstances of the Latin American church, above all out of its shortage of priests. They are networks of small communities whose worship centres around reflection on the relationship of scripture and daily life. For the most part they exist within the institutional church, and indeed depend upon the support of the hierarchy for protection from their frequently predatory civil governments. The literature on BCCs is growing apace, but the following works provide a useful introduction: Penny Lernoux, *Cry of the People* (London: Penguin Books, 1982); Thomas C. Bruneau, *The Church in Brazil* (Austin, Texas: University of Texas Press, 1982), especially chapter eight; and John Eagleson and Sergio Torres, eds., *The Challenge of Basic Christian Communities* (Maryknoll, NY: Orbis Books, 1981).

Bibliography

Primary Sources

Works by Hegel
The Christian Religion. Edited and translated by Peter C. Hodgson. AAR
  Texts and Translations Series, no. 2. Missoula, MT: Scholars Press, 1979.
Early Theological Writings. Translated by T. M. Knox, with an introduction
  and fragments translated by Richard Kroner. Philadelphia: University
  of Pennsylvania Press, 1971.
Enzyklopädie der philosophischen Wissenschaften im Grundrisse. Edited by
  Friedhelm Nicolin and Otto Pöggeler. Seventh edition. Hamburg:
  Felix Meiner Verlag, 1969.
Grundlinien der Philosophie des Rechts. Edited by Johannes Hoffmeister.
  Hamburg: Felix Meiner Verlag, 1955.
Gesammelte Werke. Edited by the Rheinisch-Westfalischen Akademie der
  Wissenschaften. Hamburg: Felix Meiner Verlag, 1968 — .
*Hegel's Logic, Being Part One of the Encyclopaedia of the Philosophical
  Sciences* (1830). Translated by William Wallace, with a foreword by
  J. N. Findlay. Oxford: Clarendon Press, 1975.
*Hegel's Philosophy of Mind, Being Part Three of the Encyclopaedia of the
  Philosophical Sciences* (1830). Translated by William Wallace, together
  with the *Zusätze* in Boumann's text (1845), translated by A. V. Miller,
  with a foreword by J. N. Findlay. Oxford: Clarendon Press, 1971.
Hegel's Philosophy of Nature. Translated by A. V. Miller, with a foreword
  by J. N. Findlay. Oxford: Clarendon Press, 1970.
Hegel's Philosophy of Right. Translated with notes by T. M. Knox. London:
  Oxford University Press, 1967.
Hegel's Political Writings. Translated by T. M. Knox, with an introductory
  essay by Z. A. Pelczynski. Oxford: Clarendon Press, 1964.
Hegel's Science of Logic. Translated by A. V. Miller, with a foreword by
  J. N. Findlay. London: Allen and Unwin, 1969.
Hegel's System of Ethical Life and First Philosophy of Spirit. Edited and
  translated by H. S. Harris and T. M. Knox. Albany, NY: State Univer-
  sity of New York Press, 1979.
Hegels theologische Jugendschriften. Edited by Hermann Nohl. Tübingen:
  J. C. B. Mohr, 1907.
Jenaer Realphilosophie. Edited by Johannes Hoffmeister. Hamburg: Felix
  Meiner Verlag, 1967.

Lectures on the Philosophy of Religion. 3 vols. Translated by E. G. Speirs and J. B. Sanderson. New York: Humanities Press, 1962.

Phänomenologie des Geistes. Edited by Johannes Hoffmeister. Hamburg: Felix Meiner Verlag, 1952.

The Phenomenology of Mind. Translated, with an introduction and notes by J. B. Baillie. New York: Harper and Row, 1967.

The Philosophy of History. Translated by J. Sibree, with a preface by Charles Hegel, and a new introduction by C. J. Friedrich. New York: Dover, 1956.

Sämtliche Werke: Jubiläumsausgabe in zwanzig Bänder. Edited by Hermann Glockner. Stuttgart: Fr. Frommanns Verlag, 1958.

System der Sittlichkeit. Edited by Georg Lasson. 2nd edition. Hamburg: Felix Meiner Verlag, 1923.

Vorlesungen über die Philosophie der Religion. Edited by Georg Lasson 4 vols. in two. Hamburg: Felix Meiner Verlag, 1925–30.

Secondary Sources

Books

Althusser, Louis, and Balibar, Etienne. *Reading Capital.* London: NLB, 1970.

Alves, Rubem. *A Theology of Human Hope.* St. Meinrad, Indiana: Abbey Press, 1975.

Asveld, Paul. *La pensée religieuse du jeune Hegel: liberté et alienation.* Louvain: Publications Universitaires, 1953.

Avineri, Shlomo. *Hegel's Theory of the Modern State.* London: Cambridge University Press, 1972.

———. *The Social and Political Thought of Karl Marx.* Cambridge: Cambridge University Press, 1968.

Barion, Jacob. *Hegel und die marxistische Staatslehre.* Bonn: Bouvier, 1963.

Barth, Karl. *Protestant Theology in the Nineteenth Century.* London: SCM, 1972.

Berger, Peter L. *The Sacred Canopy: Elements of a Sociological Theory of Religion.* New York: Doubleday, 1967.

Brito, Emilio. *Hegel et la tache actuelle de la christologie.* Paris: Editions Lethielleux, 1979.

Bruaire, Claude. *Logique et religion chretienne dans la philosophie de Hegel.* Paris: Editions du Seuil.

Bruneau, Thomas C. *The Church in Brazil.* Austin, Texas: University of Texas Press, 1982.

Chapelle, Albert. *Hegel et la religion.* 3 vols. Paris: Editions Universitaires, 1963.

Christensen, Darrel E., ed. *Hegel and the Philosophy of Religion.* The Hague: Martinus Nijhoff, 1970.

Clark, Malcolm. *Logic and System: A Study of the Transition from Vorstellung to Thought in the Philosophy of Hegel.* The Hague: Martinus Nijhoff, 1971.

Colletti, Lucio. *Marxism and Hegel.* London: NLB, 1973.

Crites, Stephen D. *In the Twilight of Christendom: Hegel versus Kierkegaard on Faith and History.* Chambersburg, Penn.: American Academy of Religion, 1972.

———. *The Problem of the "Positivity" of the Gospel in the Hegelian Dialectic of Alienation and Reconciliation.* Unpublished Ph.D. dissertation, Yale, 1961.

Eagleson, John and Torres, Sergio, eds. *The Challenge of Basic Christian Communities.* Maryknoll, NY: Orbis Press, 1981.

Edwards, David L. *The "Honest to God" Debate: Some Reactions to the Book, "Honest to God."* Philadelphia: Westminster Press, 1963.

Fackenheim, Emil L. *Encounters Between Judaism and Modern Philosophy: A Preface to Future Jewish Thought.* New York: Basic Book Inc., 1973.

———. *God's Presence in History: Jewish Affirmations and Philosophical Reflections.* New York: New York University Press, 1970.

———. *Metaphysics and Historicity.* Milwaukee: Marquette University Press, 1961.

———. *The Religious Dimension in Hegel's Thought.* Bloomington, Indiana: Indiana University Press, 1967.

Farley, Edward. *Ecclesial Man.* Philadelphia: Fortress Press, 1976.

Feuerbach, Ludwig. *Gesammelte Werke.* Edited by Werner Schuffenhauer. Berlin: Akademie Verlag, 1970.

Gadamer, Hans-Georg. *Hegel's Dialectic.* New Haven: Yale University Press, 1976.

Gehler, Klaus and Schaeffler, Richard. *Einsichten: Gerhard Kruger zum 60. Geburtstag.* Frankfurt-am-Main: Vittorio Klostermann, 1962.

Gisel, Pierre. *Vérité et Histoire: la théologie dans la modernité.* Editions Beauchesne, 1975.

Gogarten, Friedrich. *Despair and Hope for Our Time.* Philadelphia and Boston: Pilgrim Press, 1970.

Green, Michael. *The Truth of God Incarnate.* Grand Rapids: Eerdmans, 1977.

Habermas, Jürgen. *Communication and the Evolution of Society.* Boston: Beacon Press, 1976.

Herbert, Karl, ed. *Christliche Freiheit im Dienst am Menschen.* Frankfurt-am-Main: Verlag Otto Lembeck, 1972.

Hick, John, ed. *The Myth of God Incarnate.* Philadelphia: Westminster Press, 1977.

Hyppolite, Jean. *Studies on Marx and Hegel*. New York: Harper and Row, Torchbook edn., 1969.
Iljin, Ivan. *Die Philosophie Hegels also kontemplative Gotteslehre*. Bern: A. Francke Verlag, 1946.
Jaeschke, Walter. *Die Suche nach den eschatologischen Wurzeln der Geschichtsphilosophie: eine historische Kritik der Säkularisierungsthese*. Beitrage zur evangelischen Theologie, vol. 76. Munich: Chr. Kaiser Verlag, 1976.
Kaufman, Walter, ed. *Hegel's Political Philosophy*. New York: Atherton Press, 1970.
Kehl, Medard. *Kirche als Institution: zur theologische Begrundung des institutionellen Charakters der Kirche in der neueren deutschsprachigen katholischen Ekklesiologie*. Frankfurter theologische Studien, vol. 22. Frankfurt-am-Main: Joseph Knecht, 1976.
Kelly, Armstrong. *Hegel's Retreat from Eleusis: Studies in Political Thought*. Princeton: Princeton University Press, 1978.
— — —. *Idealism, Politics and History: Sources of Hegelian Thought*. Cambridge: Cambridge University Press, 1969.
Koch, Traugott, *Differenz und Versohnung: eine Interpretation der Theologie G. W. F. Hegels nach seiner Wissenschaft der Logik*. Gütersloh: Verlaghaus Gerd Mohn, 1967.
Küng, Hans. *Menschwerdung Gottes: eine Einfuhrung in Hegels theologisches Denken also Prolegomena zu einer kunftigen Christologie*. Freiburg: Herder, 1970.
Lauer, Quentin. *Essays in Hegelian Dialectic*. New York: Fordham University Press, 1977.
— — —. *Hegel's Concept of God*. Albany: SUNY, 1982.
— — —. *Hegel's Idea of Philosophy*. New York: Fordham University Press, 1971.
Lernoux, Penny. *Cry of the People*. London: Penguin Books, 1982.
Löwith, Karl. *Meaning in History*. Chicago: University of Chicago Press, 1949.
Luckmann, Thomas. *The Invisible Religion: the Problem of Religion in Modern Society*. New York: Macmillan, 1967.
Marcuse, Herbert. *Reason and Revolution*. Boston: Beacon Press, 1960.
Marsch, Wolf-Dieter. *Gegenwart Christi in der Gesellschaft: eine Studie zu Hegels Dialektik*. Munich: Chr. Kaiser Verlag, 1965.
Martin, David. *The Religious and the Secular: Studies in Secularisation*. New York: Schocken Books, 1969.
Marx, Karl. *Critique of Hegel's Philosophy of Right*. Edited with an introduction and notes by Joseph O'Malley. London: Cambridge University Press, 1970.
— — —. *The Essential Writings*. Edited by Frederic L. Bender, New York: Harper and Row, 1972.

————. *Writings of the Young Marx on Philosophy and Society*. Edited and translated by Lloyd D. Easton and Kurt H. Guddat. Garden City, NY: Doubleday Anchor, 1967.

Maurer, Reinhart Klemens. *Hegel und das Ende der Geschichte*. Stuttgart: W. Kohlhammer, 1965.

Metz, Johann-Baptist. *Theology of the World*. New York: Herder and Herder, 1969.

Miranda, José. *Marx and the Bible*. Maryknoll, NY: Orbis Press, 1975.

Möller, Joseph. *Der Geist und das Absolute*. Paderborn: Verlag Ferdinand Schöningh, 1951.

Ottmann, Henning. *Individuum und Gemeinschaft bei Hegel. Bd. 1: Hegel im Spiegel der Interpretationen*. Berlin, New York: Walter de Gruyter, 1977.

Pannenberg, Wolfhart. *The Idea of God and Human Freedom*. Philadelphia: Westminster Press, 1973.

Pelczynski, Zbigniew Andrzey, ed. *Hegel's Political Philosophy: Problems and Perspectives*. Cambridge University Press, 1971.

Pfleiderer, Otto. *The Development of Theology in Germany since Kant*. Translated by J. Frederick Smith. New York: Macmillan, 1890.

Rahner, Karl. *Theological Investigations IV*. Baltimore: Helicon, 1966.

Robinson, J. A. T. *Honest to God*. Philadelphia: Westminster Press, 1963.

Rosenzweig, Franz. *Hegel und der Staat*. 2 vols. in one. Aalen: Scientia Verlag, 1962.

Rupp, George. *Christologies and Cultures*. The Hague: Mouton, 1974.

Schillebeeckx, Edward. *God: The Future of Man*. New York: Sheed and Ward, 1968.

————. *The Understanding of Faith: Interpretation and Criticism*. London: The Catholic Book Club, 1975.

Schmidt, Erik. *Hegels System der Theologie*. Berlin: Walter de Gruyter, 1974.

Segundo, Juan Luis. *The Liberation of Theology*. London: Gill and Macmillan, 1977.

Shiner, Larry, *The Secularization of History: An Introduction to the Theology of F. Gogarten*. Nashville and New York: Abingdon Press, 1966.

Sobrino, Jon. *Christology at the Crossroads: A Latin-American Approach*. London: SCM, 1978.

Soelle, Dorothee. *Christ the Representative*. Philadelphia: Fortress Press, 1967.

————. *Political Theology*. Philadelphia: Fortress Press, 1974.

Splett, Jorg. *Die Trinitätslehre G. W. F. Hegels*. Freiburg-Munich: Karl Alber Verlag, 1965.

Taylor, Charles, *Hegel*. Cambridge: Cambridge University Press, 1975.

————. *Hegel and Modern Society*. Cambridge: Cambridge University Press, 1979.

Theunissen, Michael. *Hegels Lehre vom absoluten Geist als theologisch-politischer Traktat.* Berlin: Walter de Gruyter, 1970.
Tillich, Paul. *Theology of Culture.* Oxford: Oxford University Press, 1975.
Walsh, William H. *Hegelian Ethics.* London: Macmillan, 1969.
Xhaufflaire, Marcel. *Feuerbach et la théologie de la secularisation.* Paris: Editions du Cerf, 1970.
Yerkes, James. *The Christology of Hegel.* Albany, NY: SUNY Press, 1982.

Articles

Fackenheim, Emil L. "On the Actuality of the Rational and the Rationality of the Actual." *Review of Metaphysics* 23 (1970): 690–698.
Gisel, Pierre. "Finitude, Temporalité et Contingence." *Revue de Théologie et de Philosophie* III (1979): 217–231.
Hebblethwaite, Brian. "The Property of the Doctrine of the Incarnation as a Way of Interpreting Christ." *Scottish Journal of Theology* 33 (1980): 201–222.
Jonas, Hans. "Heidegger and Theology." *Review of Metaphysics* 18 (1964): 207–233.
Kaufmann, Walter. "Hegel's Early Antitheological Phase." *Philosophical Review* 63 (1954): 3–18.
— — —. "The Hegel Myth and Its Method." *Philosophical Review* 60 (1951): 459–486.
Kroner, Richard. "System und Geschichte bei Hegel." *Logos* 20 (1930): 243–258.
Müller, G. E. "The Hegel Legend of 'Thesis, Antithesis and Synthesis'." *Journal of the History of Ideas* 19 (1958): 411–414.
Müller, Max. "Über Sinn und Sinngefährdung des menschlichen Daseins." *Philosophisches Jahrbuch* 74 (1966): 1–29.
Rohrmoser, Günter. "Die theologische Voraussetzungen der Hegelschen Lehre vom Staat." *Hegel-Studien*, Beiheft 1 (1964): 239–245.
Schmidt, Gerhard. "Die Religion in Hegels Staat." *Philosophisches Jahrbuch* 74 (1967): 294–309.
Schweitzer, C. A. "Zur Methode der Hegelinterpretation. Eine Entgegnung auf Karl Löwiths 'Hegels Aufhebung der christlichen Religion'." *Neue Zeitschrift fur systematische Theologie und Religionsphilosophie* 5 (1963): 248–262.

Index